the
POLITICS
ASSOCIATION

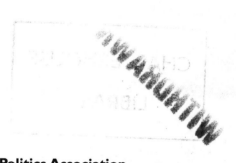

Produced for the Politics Association
Old Hall Lane
Manchester M13 0XT

Sheffield Hallam University Press
Learning Centre
City Campus
Howard Street
Sheffield S1 1WB

Designed and typeset by
Design Studio, Learning Centre, Sheffield Hallam University

The views expressed by the writers in this series are personal ones.
They do not necessarily represent those of the Politics Association
or Sheffield Hallam University Press

© Rob Baggott 2000
ISBN 0 86339 848 0

 *Sheffield Hallam University*

Pressure Groups and the Policy Process

by **Rob Baggott**

Dedicated to **Joyce Capewell** *1912 – 2000*

About the author
Rob Baggott is Professor of Public Policy at De Montfort University,
Leicester. His research interests include pressure group politics, health
policy and social policy. He has published a number of other books: *Alcohol,
Politics and Social Policy* (Avebury, 1990), *Pressure Groups: A Question of
Interest* (PAVIC, 1994), *Pressure Groups Today* (Manchester University
Press, 1995), *Health and Health Care in Britain* (Macmillan, 1994, second
edition, 1998) and *Public Health: Policy and Politics* (Macmillan, 2000).

Acknowledgements:
I would like to thank Duncan Watts for his editorial advice and guidance,
not to mention his tact and patience. Thanks too to Tracey Dodman for her
assistance with research on the consultation process. I would also like to
thank the staff of the House of Commons Information Office for details of
draft bills and special Standing Committees.

Titles available in this series:
October 1999
British Government and Politics: a Comparative Guide (core text)
January 2000
Britain and the European Union: an Uneasy Partnership
British Electoral Systems: Achieving a Sense of Proportion
British Voters: the Changing Basis of Party Choice
Parliament in an Age of Reform
The Changing Constitution: Evolution or Revolution?
Whitehall and the Civil Service: Issues for the Millennium and Beyond
September 2000
Democracy in Britain: Theory and Practice
Devolved Great Britain: the New Governance of England, Scotland and Wales
The Mass Media: Political Communication in Britain Today

Contents

List of Exhibits

Welcome to the world of pressure groups

I n this short introductory chapter I briefly set out the main
characteristics of the pressure group world – the large number of groups
and their diversity.

ASK YOURSELF

- Why are there so many pressure groups and why are they so diverse?
- What difficulties does this diversity present for those studying pressure-group politics?

MAIN TEXT

Pressure groups are an important part of the political landscape in several respects. First, there are lots of them. The Directory of British Associations lists over 7000 nationally recognised associations in Britain[1], though this figure is almost certainly an underestimate of the actual number of pressure groups in existence. Some groups are transient and do not exist for long enough to be included in such directories. Others operate at a local rather than a national level. Indeed it seems that there is a great deal of pressure group activity at the local level: a study of local politics in Birmingham in the 1970s found over 4000 organisations in that city alone[2].

Secondly, pressure groups are diverse, reflecting the multitifarious interests, preferences and values of the nation. Some groups are rather obscure, focusing on highly specialised issues. Examples include the British Toilet Association, the English Collective of Prostitutes, the Lancashire Cheese Association, the Impotence Association, the Zip Fastener Association, and the Tall Persons Club of Great Britain. These smaller and less well-known organisations contrast with the giants of the pressure group world, which

1

are so firmly rooted in the public's mind that they are commonly referred to simply by their initials – such as the BMA, the TUC, the CBI, and the NFU. These are huge organisations, employing hundreds of people, with membership lists running into tens of thousands. They have the resources to match those of the government agencies they are seeking to influence. They are highly professionalised and skilled in the art of lobbying. Their involvement in politics is extensive and continuous.

For the smaller fry, involvement in the political process is more sporadic. Examples might include a local golf club lobbying against plans to build a ring road; a parents' and toddlers' group campaigning to keep playgroup facilities open, a recreational club for the elderly arguing the case for a pedestrian crossing on a busy road, a residents' association opposing plans to build a waste incinerator nearby, and so on. Such groups represent an important channel through which people can participate in decisions about their welfare and wellbeing.

So potentially at least pressure groups have an important representative function and this is the third reason why they are significant. They can act as a link between ordinary people and decision-makers. This is not to say they are always effective in this respect. As we shall see later, the representativeness of groups has been challenged. Nevertheless, most people would regard the freedom to organise and collectively represent views as an important democratic principle.

Finally, pressure group politics involves a wide range of political actors, not just the pressure groups themselves. Businesses and public service providers are not, strictly-speaking, pressure groups, but they may become involved in pressure group politics. Both small businesses and large corporations are involved in lobbying decision-makers, promoting policies which they believe will enhance their profitability. Schools and hospitals have also been engaged in lobbying, for example opposing plans to change their status or to close them down. But business organisations and public sector institutions are also the subject or target of pressure group politics. For example businesses may be lobbied by pressure group to improve their record on the environment. Schools and hospitals can also be the subject of pressure group campaigns. Under current legislation grammar schools can face campaigns to change their status by way of a local ballot and this provides an opportunity for pressure groups to put their case. For example in Ripon there was a tremendous battle between the pro and anti-grammar school lobbies, which the former won in early 2000. Meanwhile efforts to reorganise hospitals in many cities including London, Leeds and Leicester have led to opposition from pressure groups at local level.

In addition, pressure groups engage with many other parts of the political system, parties, the media, government, and Parliament. They may also operate beyond national boundaries, interacting with European institutions and international bodies such as the World Trade Organisation and the World Health Organisation. Pressure groups are involved at all stages of the policy process from raising issues and agenda setting to policy implementation and monitoring.

In short pressure groups cannot be ignored by students of the political processes. However, many of the factors which make it important to study pressure groups also cause difficulties. The number and diversity of groups (not to mention the absence of an accurate 'database' of them) makes it difficult to evaluate general patterns of behaviour and trends over time. How do we know that the 'sample' of groups we are studying reflects the characteristics of groups in general? The diversity of groups also gives rise to definitional problems. For example, even the term 'pressure group' itself has to be extremely broad in order to cover all the various types of group. We shall consider these questions in the next section.

Analysing pressure groups

INTRODUCTION

This chapter explores the problems and pitfalls of examining pressure groups and discusses how academics have tried to make sense of the pressure group world. The chapter discusses their efforts to define pressure groups and to establish typologies and classifications.

ASK YOURSELF

- Why has a single, commonly agreed definition of pressure groups not emerged?
- Is it possible in practice to clearly distinguish pressure groups from other political institutions such as political parties and government agencies?

MAIN TEXT

There is no commonly agreed definition of a pressure group. Indeed, academic writers on this subject have tended to formulate their own working definitions. Fundamentally, these definitions are similar (see Exhibit one) in that they seek to create a distinction between pressure groups and other political institutions such as political parties and government agencies.

It is frequently held that the main distinction between pressure groups and parties is that the former do not aspire to govern. How true is this? Certainly most pressure groups are concerned with the details of policymaking rather than the kind of strategic direction which one associates with effective government. But it would be wrong to see pressure groups as detached from the process of government. Indeed as will become clear later, pressure groups are closely involved in the governing process, not simply by representing interests and influencing policy, but also by undertaking functions on behalf of government.

Exhibit one
Definitions of a pressure group

Baggott: 'A pressure group is an organisation which seeks to influence the details of a comparatively small range of public policies and which is not a faction of a recognised political party'[1]

Ball and Millard: 'In general, pressure groups are social aggregates with some level of cohesion and shared aims which attempt to influence the political decision making process'[2]

Castles: 'any group attempting to bring about political change whether through government activity or not, and which is not a political party in the sense of being represented at that particular time in the legislative body.'[3]

Roberts: 'an organised group which has as one of its purposes the exercise of influence... on political institutions, for the purpose of securing unfavourable decisions or preventing unfavourable ones'.[4]

Alderman: 'those units, organised or not, of the democratic process which have a set purpose or set of purposes, but which are nonetheless neither political parties nor formal agencies of government.'[5]

Grant: 'A pressure group is an organisation which seeks as one of its functions to influence the formulation and implementation of public policy, public policy representing a set of authoritative decisions taken by the executive, the legislature, and the judiciary, and by local government and the European Community.'[6]

Distinguishing pressure groups and parties

It could be argued that the dividing line between parties and pressure groups is quite clear. Parties seek to win elections and form a government, while pressure groups do not. This sounds a simple enough distinction, but one should remember that pressure groups have in the past fielded candidates, particularly at by-elections, mainly for publicity reasons.

One of the main problems one faces when trying to distinguish parties from pressure groups is that the two types of institution are often closely interlinked. The Conservative Party, for example, is traditionally closely allied to business organisations, which help fund the party. The Labour Party has a historically close relationship with the Trades Unions, which provide finance and participate in the decision making processes within the

Party. In recent years, however, both parties have sought to publicly distance themselves from these interests in an effort to combat claims that are unduly influenced by them.

Parties are themselves often an arena for pressure group conflict. Each party represents a broad spectrum of views and these are often expressed in the form of party factions. In the Conservative Party, for example, one finds a number of factions ranging from the right wing 'No Turning Back' group of MPs, through to the moderate 'Tory Reform Group'. The Labour Party also has factions, such as Tribune, the Campaign group, and the Solidarity group of MPs. Within the parties, factions occasionally arise on a particular issue. For example, in the Labour Party conflicting views on electoral reform led to the creation within the Party of a 'Campaign for Electoral Reform' which has supported change and a 'Campaign for Electoral Success' which has opposed reform.

In most cases one can easily distinguish between pressure groups and political parties. However, where interests and causes operate through both types of institution it can be difficult to discern where party ends and where pressure group begins. This is particularly the case with 'movements' such as the Greens, the Peace Movement and the Women's movement, which transcend party and pressure-group politics.

Pressure groups and government bodies

Pressure groups are in the main private or voluntary sector organisations, funded by their own members and private donations. But many pressure groups are often more dependent on the state than at first appears. Some are funded by government. The anti-smoking group Action on Smoking and Health (ASH) receives a large proportion of its budget from the Department of Health. In addition the government gives grants totalling over £400m a year to a range of voluntary organisations. Although most of this covers the cost of providing voluntary services, such as health and social services in the community, some of it goes towards the core costs of the organisation which include research, publicity and policy work. In a sense the voluntary sector has become an extension of the state, and therefore is not strictly independent of it. Indeed government departments have on occasion threatened to withdraw funding for groups which have criticised them.

The government not only funds pressure groups, it sometimes plays a role in establishing them. For example, the National Consumer Council was set up by the government in 1975 to promote consumer interests. In 1966 the Home Office helped to establish the National Association for the Care and Resettlement of Offenders (NACRO), which has since become an authoritative pressure group on issues such as penal reform and the rehabilitation of offenders.

The distinction between government agencies and pressure groups is difficult to sustain, particularly when one realises the extent to which government agencies themselves indulge in lobbying. This is particularly true of the Quasi-government agencies or QUANGOs. Bodies such as the Commission for Racial Equality, the Equal Opportunities Commission, the Arts Council, the Countryside Agency, the Commission for Integrated Transport, often act like pressure groups, lobbying ministers, civil servants and MPs to promote their interests. Furthermore, government has established a variety of institutional settings, such as committees, task forces and forums, where government and group representatives can interact to develop policy. In these settings it is often difficult to establish where government ends and where groups begin.

The search for a definition of a pressure group based on distinctions between these institutions and parties and government bodies has become something of a parlour game. Some academics tired of this and gave up the hunt for a commonly accepted definition. Richardson and Jordan, for example, argue that it is not useful to begin with a strict definition of pressure group. They prefer to focus on the group 'process': the relationships between political organisations rather than upon the precise institutional status and organisational features of these groups.[7]. There is some advantage in this, in that it moves away from sterile debates about whether a particular institution is or is not a pressure group towards an analysis based on actual behaviour within the political process. However, there is one drawback in that potentially at least any institution that seeks to influence policy could be regarded as a pressure group and this expands the field of inquiry considerably. Indeed it could well shift the focus away from key research questions, such as how groups are organised, how they represent the public, and how they establish their legitimacy, which most would regard as central to the study of pressure groups.

But the situation is not really as polarised as it appears. Both the narrow institutional and the broader process-oriented perspectives have a valuable role to play in furthering our understanding of pressure group politics. The institutional approach emphasises the 'extra-governmental' nature of pressure groups, while the broader perspective stresses the extent to which they are embedded in the broader political process.

Types of pressure group

As noted earlier, one of the main problems faced by those who seek to understand pressure groups is their diversity. This means that it is quite difficult to generalise about groups. A number of political scientists have tried to deal with this by subdividing pressure groups into different categories (see Exhibit two).

Basically there are two kinds of group. On the one hand those which primarily pursue the self interests of their members, and whose members are drawn from a specific social group, such as an occupation, industry, trade or profession. These are known as 'interest groups' (and by some writers as functional groups or sectional groups). On the other hand there are groups which exist primarily to further what they perceive as the public interest or the interests of specific 'third party'. These groups have a more open membership and their members may be drawn from a variety of social and economic backgrounds. These are known as 'cause groups' (or, alternatively, attitude groups, promotional groups or preference groups).

Exhibit two
Types of pressure group

Interest groups	**Cause groups**
Membership *restricted* to those with a shared background or performing a common socio-economic function	Membership *open* to those who support the cause
Primarily exists to protect members' *self interests* as defined by the group	Primarily exists to further the *interests of others* or the *public interest* as defined by the group

This distinction is, however, difficult to maintain in practice. Although many groups fall clearly into one or other of the categories, some do not. Professional bodies, for example, seek to protect the interests of their members, but they also campaign on issues of public interest. For example the BMA and the Royal Colleges of Medicine have for many years called on government to take tougher action against smoking in an attempt to protect the public's health. Interest groups sometimes do pursue causes when there is no direct personal benefit to their members.

Some interest groups also establish or maintain cause groups. For example in the early seventies the Royal College of Physicians established Action on Smoking and Health (ASH) to campaign against smoking. But cause groups are not always established for altruistic reasons. Interest groups often set up cause groups as a means of pooling resources on an issue of common interest, and in an attempt to create a broader level of public support for their views. For example, in the 1980s some of the larger retailers set up 'Open Shop' to campaign for reform of the Sunday trading laws. This group not only co-ordinated the activities of the major interests involved, but was part of an attempt to mobilise public opinion in favour of Sunday trading, and it was eventually successful in promoting a change in the law.

Other typologies seek to distinguish pressure groups on the basis of their interaction with the policy process. Benewick [8] argued that there were three 'worlds' of pressure groups, each characterised by particular type of group and a certain kind of government-group relationship. The 'first world' consists of groups which have considerable political resources, are seen as legitimate by government, and have continuous access to decision-makers with whom they have a stable relationship. The 'second world' comprises groups which although not short of resources nor lacking legitimacy, have less frequent contact with government. In contrast groups in the 'third world' are not perceived as legitimate by government and do not enjoy the kind of access of groups in the first and second worlds. Unlike the other two kinds of group those in the third world seek to challenge the current balance of power. The implication of Benewick's classification is that groups in the first and second worlds will exert more influence over government policy than those in the third world. However, as Benewick himself accepts, third world groups may be important in challenging the status quo. As others have noted, this may be achieved in a number of ways, including protest campaigns (see Exhibit 7). Such groups may also be influential in shaping the perception of issues and how policies are actually implemented. For example, Ryan's study of the pressure group INQUEST noted how a 'third world group' influenced the way in which suicide deaths in legal custody were perceived and had a real impact on suicide prevention[10].

Benewick's approach is reflected in Grant's distinction between insiders and outsiders [11]. Insiders are viewed as legitimate by government and are regularly consulted whereas outsider groups lack these privileges. Within these categories Grant makes a further distinction between insiders that cultivate media support (high profile insiders) and those which do not (low profile insiders). He also describes some insider groups as 'prisoner groups' because they are dependent on government assistance or support. Similarly outsiders are divided into three categories: potential insiders, which as their name suggests could become insiders, for example by adopting a more responsible and conventional strategy. Outsiders by necessity are groups that are less skilful and knowledgeable about the political process. Ideological outsiders are groups that do not wish to become insiders because of their radical aims or their preference for direct action.

Although Grant's typology has proved useful, it has been criticised on a number of grounds. First, it assumes that insider groups are more influential than outsider groups over policy. This is not necessarily the case. Insider status may constrain groups who oppose government policy but do not wish to lose their privileged status. Secondly, outsider groups can exert influence over public attitudes and the political agenda and may ultimately have an impact on government policy.

A second criticism is that access to government is more open than Grant's model appears to suggest. According to Maloney and colleagues [12], the key distinction is not between insider and outsiders but between the different types of insider group. They distinguish between core, specialist and peripheral insiders. Core insiders are seen by government as important sources of information across the range of a broad policy area (eg: health, agriculture). Specialist insiders are highly regarded within a smaller, more closely defined policy field (eg: food safety). Peripheral insiders have limited access to the consultation process and have a fairly marginal impact on policy. Maloney and colleagues argue that research should focus on why certain groups are influential once they have met the fairly minimal requirements for insider status. However they do recognise the existence of outsider groups, identifying two types; outsiders by ideology (whose goals are incompatible with government) and outsiders by choice (which do not wish to engage with government).

Maloney and colleagues echo a point made by Whiteley and Winyard [13] that Grant conflates two different characteristics of pressure groups: strategy and structure. A group may have insider status but may well adopt a strategy that involves contact with the media and Parliament. Indeed studies of pressure group activity have shown that groups with 'insider status' are actually more frequently in touch with Parliament than outsider groups [14].

Whiteley and Winyard in their study of the poverty lobby adopted a fourfold classification relating to four characteristics: strategy (groups were either *focused* on Whitehall or adopted a more *open* strategy); support (groups were either *representative*, consisting of a group within the community such as disabled people, or they were *promotional*, speaking on their behalf); status (groups either *accepted* by policy makers or *non accepted*); and aims (groups were either primarily *lobbying* or primarily providing *services* for their members/clients). They then classified groups according to these characteristics. The most common profiles were OPAL (Open-Promotional-Accepted-Lobbying) and FRAS (Focused-Representational-Accepted-Lobbying), the former profile was found among the more effective pressure groups in the poverty field.

Another approach has been to move away from classifications of groups towards classification of policy networks within which groups operate. Some argue that the relationships between actors (government agencies, pressure groups and others) should be the focus of research. Writers such as Rhodes, Marsh and Smith [15] identify different types of policy network, the configuration of which has implications for policy outcomes. The two main types of network are policy communities and issue networks. Policy communities have a small and exclusive membership, are characterised by close, continuous and stable relationships between participants, there is high level of consensus and trust and considerable interdependence between government agencies and groups. Issue networks in contrast contain a larger number of participants, are characterised by instability and conflict, there is a lower degree of trust though some agreement is possible, relationships are not close and continuous and there is little interdependence between government and groups

Policy network analysis has been used to explain policy developments, though it has been criticised for its failure to explain the dynamics of change (see [16]). The academic debates are quite complex. Nevertheless, they have revealed what needs to be investigated further. Namely how government manages the processes of representation and consultation to allow different kinds of interaction to take place. And secondly how groups are able to enter policy arenas and use their position to influence the policy process. It is worth noting in this context, an American study [17] which examines how excluded groups can challenge the status quo by setting new agendas which place a premium on their skills and resources. This can result in the creation of new institutional structures which incorporate these groups and their ideas and interests.

CONCLUSION

There are many different approaches to defining and classifying pressure groups. In recent years the emphasis has moved away from basic approaches that seek to distinguish groups on the basis of their organisational features towards those focused on behaviour or position within the political system. There is still much debate about how to define and classify groups, with established approaches (such as Grant's insider/outsider typology) coming under increasing attack.

Pressure groups and policy making

INTRODUCTION

Pressure groups interact with the political process in an effort to influence policy. But the concept of policy is itself broad and covers a wide range of decision and opinion forming arenas. In this chapter I shall discuss why groups get involved in the policy process and the extent and range of their involvement.

ASK YOURSELF

- In what sense do groups seek to influence policy?
- How can we judge the 'influence' of pressure groups?
- What are the main stages of the policy process?
- What are the main 'pressure points' that groups seek to target?

MAIN TEXT

Pressure groups undertake a wide range of activities, not all of which are political. These include the provision of services to members, as in the case of trade unions, employers' organisations and professional associations. Many pressure groups, such as companies, voluntary organisations and charities, deliver goods and services to the public or to specific client groups. These services are important, and can have a bearing on how these organisations are perceived by both government and the general public. Furthermore, the internal workings of such organisations, and in particular how they determine their priorities, are of interest to political scientists. However, students of political behaviour are mainly interested in how pressure groups interact with the political process. They are particularly keen to learn about how groups influence policy decisions.

Pressure groups seek to influence the policymaking process in several ways. The precise tactics which they use to this end are discussed later. For the moment, though, it is important to look at the nature of pressure group influence, and the focus of their activities.

Influence

There are three senses in which pressure groups seek influence. First of all, they attempt to influence the decisions of those who make policy. This could take the form of an amendment to legislation, or an allocation of resources to a public spending programme. It could also relate to decisions about policy implementation at national or subnational level. Secondly, pressure groups try to influence the government's political agenda. This means getting the government to consider issues where a group is keen to see policy develop and by the same token to ignore issues which pose a threat to its interests or preferences. Thirdly, pressure groups try to influence the attitudes of the public with regard to those issues which the groups feel strongly about.

It is usually believed that the most important form of influence is the first - influence over decisions. But issues have to get on to the political agenda or attract public concern before decisions can be made. Influencing the political agenda and the climate of opinion should not therefore be ignored. For example, during the 1980s, the environmental lobby was extremely successful in bringing to the public's attention issues such as global warming, ozone depletion, CFCs (Chlorofluorocarbons), deforestation, air pollution, overuse of fertilisers and pesticides, the disposal of toxic waste, and acid rain. As these issues were thrust on to the political agenda, particularly in the industrialised democracies, governments had to respond to these concerns. They did so by formulating international agreements on CFCs, so-called greenhouse gases, biological diversity and sustainable development. In the UK this was followed through by environmental protection legislation, a sustainable development plan and strategies to cut pollution. Although these policies were criticised for not going far enough to protect the environment, it is doubtful that they would have emerged at all without the efforts of environmental campaigners [1].

Influence can be judged on the basis short-term or long-term perspective. Some pressure groups have achieved influence only after many years of campaigning. For example, the Abortion Law Reform Association lobbied for 40 years before abortion was eventually legalised in 1967. Yet even this hard won victory has been challenged in recent years by countervailing pressures of the anti-abortion lobby, which was successful in pressing for a reduction in the time limit during which legal abortions can be performed. Pressure groups which are successful in the short-term may not be judged so in the future. Again on the issue of Sunday trading, the Keep Sunday Special campaign was initially successful in impeding the governments deregulation plans during the mid 1980s. But eventually the pressure for more liberal trading hours on Sunday, as noted earlier, resulted in a change in the law.

Pressure points

When trying to influence policy, pressure groups are aware of a range of 'pressure points' where issues are raised and debated, where policies are formed and decisions made. These 'pressure points' are the principal focal points for pressure group lobbying.(see Exhibit three)

National government includes institutions such as Parliament, government departments and agencies, the political parties, and the cabinet system, and individuals such as ministers, civil servants, and policy advisors. In the UK, legitimate power has been concentrated at national level, and local government is relatively weak. Most observers agree that during the 1980s

---

Exhibit three
Pressure points

Global government	**UK national government**	**Private organisations**
UN institutions	The Executive	Business organisations
Other international bodies	Parliament	Political Parties
Foreign governments		The Media
	Sub-national government	
European government	Devolved assemblies	**Other pressure groups**
Council of Ministers	Regional agencies	
European Commission	Local authorities	
European Parliament		
European Court of Justice		
Other member states		

and 1990s there was a greater degree of centralisation, as reflected in controls on local government, and the replacement of some of their functions by non-elected bodies appointed by ministers. This appears to be part of a longer term trend whereby national authorities have regulated or taken over functions which have formerly been in the domain of local government. More recently, however, there have been important constitutional changes which may well alter this. Devolution in Scotland and devolved assemblies in Wales and Northern Ireland have created new centres of power to which pressure groups have been attracted, creating the prospect of a less centralised system of pressure group lobbying and the likelihood of different political agendas and policies within the UK. Furthermore the possible introduction of regional assemblies may have a similar effect within England itself, devolving some decisions downwards and changing the lobbying strategies of pressure groups as a result.

Local government includes local authorities, and other local and regional agencies, such as the health authorities for example. Although as suggested above the power and status of local government declined in the latter part of the twentieth century, pressure groups continue to thrive at local level. This perhaps illustrates that local authorities still matter and that they continue to make many important decisions.

European Institutions include the Council of Ministers, the European Parliament, European Commission and the European Court of Justice. As a member of the European Union, the UK is bound by decisions made by these institutions. Pressure groups now realise the importance of these institutions in shaping domestic policies and a survey undertaken in 1991 found that 12% had established a European office as a base for lobbying, a proportion which is likely to have increased since[2]. Increasingly British pressure groups have formed alliances with similar groups in other countries. In some cases this has led to the formation of European-wide pressure groups (see Exhibit four).

Other organisations which represent a target for pressure group lobbying include the political parties (already discussed in chapter 1 and on p62-3), mass media, business organisations and even pressure groups themselves. Most pressure groups are keen to use media to raise awareness about the issues they feel strongly about. But media organisation also have their own agenda and seek to advance and inhibit particular issues. Companies are often the target for lobbying, particularly the large corporations which have enormous economic power, such as the large manufacturing companies, the former nationalised corporations, the major financial service institutions, and the big supermarket chains. Sometimes groups are themselves a battleground for pressure group conflict. A recent example is the case of the National Trust, which is itself a major player in the conservation lobby. For a number of years the National Trust has been an important arena for conflict between the pro-and anti-hunting lobby. The latter have operated within the National Trust to seek a ban to prevent hunting on National Trust land. In 1997 these campaigners secured a ban on stag hunting, a move which the pro-hunt lobby vowed to overturn.

A pressure group must focus on those institutions where decisions affecting its preferences or interests are being made. This varies according to the nature of the issue concerned. In some cases efforts may be best directed towards local government. In others, national government or European institutions may be the best target for the pressure group.

Exhibit four
Pressure groups and Europe

The increasing influence of European Institutions over domestic policy has convinced many British pressure groups of the importance of lobbying these institutions. Following the extension of the scope and power of European Institutions in the Single European Act (1987), the Masstricht Treaty (1992) and more recently the Amsterdam Treaty (1997), groups realised that it was vital to influence decision-making at the European level. They also realised that they could not depend on lobbying national government alone, in the hope that this would result in an outcome in their favour. The extension of qualified majority voting meant that even if national governments could be persuaded to support the group's policy they could be outvoted. Another problem was that national governments, though apparently persuaded by a groups arguments, might be prepared to 'sell out' on one issue in order to gain concessions from their European partners.

Another reason for the expansion in lobbying at the European level was the relative openness of the European institutions to representations made by pressure groups. Indeed there was a stark contrast with the experience of many British pressure groups during the 1980s, which felt that their government did not particularly welcome their views. These included trade unions, environmental groups, welfare groups and local government associations. During this period these groups expanded their European activities considerably and won a number of significant victories against the British Government's domestic policies. For example, during the latter part of the 1980s, Friends of the Earth and other environmental groups lobbied the European Commission over Britain's exemptions from the European water quality directives, which resulted in British Government accepting these standards.

Among the European Union Institutions, the *Council of Ministers* is the supreme decision making body. This can only really be influenced by lobbying national governments. However, there is a Committee of Permanent Representatives (COREPER), which consists of civil servants drawn from the member states. These individuals play a vital role in the negotiations which take place behind the scenes between member states in an effort to reach decisions. But it is generally accepted that they are accessible only to the most powerful lobby groups.

The *European Commission* is more accessible and is indeed the major target for most interests. The Commission prepares the way for legislation and other decisions. Good contacts with various Directorates in the Commission is vital if groups are to be fully aware of policy developments.

The European Parliament now has much more power than in the past. largely through the co-decision procedures, which mean that legislation can be referred to a joint body of the Parliament and the Council of Ministers to seek a compromise. In extreme circumstances Parliament can actually veto legislation if it can muster an absolute majority against the measure.

Finally one should not forget the *Court of Justice*, which is the supreme court for interpreting European law. Although the Court is not lobbied in the conventional sense, pressure groups can help to bring a legal challenge to domestic law on the grounds that it contravenes European law. In the 1980s and 1990s, for example British trade unions and welfare pressure groups supported a number of cases on issues such as equal pay, carers' rights, workers' rights, retirement ages, and maternity rights, which led to changes in British law.

Increasingly British pressure groups have joined forces with similar groups in other European countries. This has taken the form of informal alliances to lobby on a particular issue, and in some cases has led the formation of European-wide groups (Euro-groups). Examples include UNICE, which represents employers in Europe, the European Environmental Bureau (EEB), an association of national environmental organisations, ETUC, the European Trade Union Conference, and BEUC, the European Group of Consumer Associations. In one survey undertaken in 1991, around three quarters of British groups were members of a European-wide pressure group [2].

As some commentators have noted, the creation of greater European integration has not made the nation state redundant[3]. Pressure groups must lobby at several levels in order to influence policy. A good example is anti-smoking policy. Since the early 1970s the British government has regulated the advertising of tobacco through voluntary agreements with the industry. Anti-smoking groups believed this to be a weak form of regulation, and that all tobacco advertising should be banned as a means of discouraging smoking. These groups lobbied the European Commission and the European Parliament, with some success. In 1989 the European Commission imposed stronger and larger health warnings on cigarette packets, against the wishes of the British government. Following this the European Commission, supported by the European Parliament, sought to ban all forms of tobacco advertising, which provoked furious opposition from the tobacco industry. The UK government was also opposed to this, but its position was reversed by the Blair government, which adopted a tougher stance on smoking than its predecessor. Following agreement at the European level, a comprehensive ban on advertising and sponsorship was announced, to be implemented in stages by 2006. However, there was much anger in the anti-smoking lobby that some high profile forms of advertising, notably tobacco sponsorship of international sporting events such as motor racing, had been given a longer period of grace before the ban came into force. It then became known that a donation had been made to the Labour Party prior to the General Election by Bernie Ecclestone, the Vice-President of the FIA, the association representing Formula One Racing. Both Ecclestone and Labour strenuously denied that the money was linked to influence over policy and in the fact the money was subsequently returned. Meanwhile at the domestic level the Blair Government announced its own ban on tobacco advertising to come into force in the year 2000. At the time of writing, amid protests from the anti-smoking lobby. the tobacco industry has been given additional time to comply with the ban. Meanwhile the industry launched a legal challenge both to the European-wide ban and the UK legislation.

Pressure groups tend to gravitate towards established centres of decision making. But they will not necessarily be able to gain access to these arenas. Even if they do, it is by no means certain that they will actually exert any influence over policy. The extent to which pressure groups are effective in these respects depends on three sets of factors:

- Resources
- Political contacts
- The political environment and circumstances

The remainder of this book will explore these factors further.

CONCLUSION

Pressure groups seek to influence policy in a variety of ways. They seek to influence the political agenda, the legislative process and the implementation of policy. There are a number of pressure points which they can address. They will approach these pressure points on the basis of their knowledge about where key decisions are being made and in view of their resources, political contacts and other circumstances.

Pressure group resources

INTRODUCTION

Pressure groups have a variety of resources which they can employ when lobbying. In this chapter I explore these various resources under the three headings: organisational; economic; and social.

ASK YOURSELF

- What kinds of resources do pressure groups possess?
- How might these resources be useful when engaging in lobbying?
- Which resources are the most important and why?
- Is the allocation of resources between groups fairly equal or are they unequally distributed, and what are the implications of the distribution of resources?

MAIN TEXT

Organisation

It almost goes without saying that good organisation is a vital resource. Indeed many interests within society are underrepresented because they face problems of organisation. Unemployed people, for example, are very poorly organised. Since the late seventies unemployment has affected a large proportion of the population, and for many it has blighted their lives. Yet there is no coherent, well-organised pressure group to harness this depth of feeling. As a result unemployed people are a weak group politically. Similarly, chronically ill people find it difficult to organise. Pressure group activity is time-consuming and hard work. Those who are ill find it difficult to form and maintain their own groups. They are often isolated by their illness and find it difficult to organise. Even so, groups representing sick people do emerge. Sometimes they are run by carers, relatives or others seeking to promote their interests on their behalf. But there are groups which include sufferers or former patients among their membership, for example the British Diabetic Association, the Haemophilia Society and National Kidney Federation.

In a general sense 'good organisation' means that a group's economic and political resources are utilised efficiently, and in line with a clearly formulated strategy. Features of an effective organisation include a coherent decision making process; high quality staff; and adequate financial resources. There is little consensus on what makes an effective organisation in the field of pressure groups. However, there is some support for the view that a small, highly centralised and highly professionalised organisation will be a more effective lobbying body than a large, decentralised, membership-based group, with cumbersome decision-making procedures [1]. However, it is very much a case of 'swings and roundabouts'. Although smaller bodies may be more flexible and can respond quickly to events, the larger representative bodies can be seen as more legitimate particularly where they are able to articulate a broad and diverse range of opinions across a particular sector.

However, it is important that a pressure group operates coherently as a political force. Divisions of opinion between members, and between the leaders and the rank and file must be minimised, if not eliminated. Such divisions can be very damaging to a pressure group, and may even lead to the formation of a breakaway or splinter group. For example, this happened to the National Union of Miners both in 1926, and in the 1984/5 miners' strike, in the latter case leading to the formation of the Union of Democratic Mineworkers.

Good leadership is important both to prevent serious divisions and to focus pressure groups on their main objectives. Pressure group leaders need to be effective organisers. But increasingly they also have to project the image of the group in the media. For this task, they must have charisma or personal appeal. They also require political skills in order to argue, negotiate with and persuade decision-makers.

Small wonder then that pressure group politics is seen as a considerable breeding ground for future politicians, particularly in the Labour Party. Current MPs who have worked for pressure groups before standing for Parliament include Frank Field (Child Poverty Action Group), Harriet Harman (National Council for Civil Liberties, now known simply as Liberty) and Joan Ruddock (Campaign for Nuclear Disarmament). It is also interesting to note that pressure groups can provide employment for former politicians who are no longer in Parliament. For example, after losing his seat in the 1987 General Election, Alf Dubs became the director of the British Refugee Council. Another example is the former MP Roger King, who joined the Society of Motor Manufacturers and Traders after being defeated in the 1992 General Election. Former ministers and civil servants may also join pressure groups after they have retired or resigned. Their knowledge of the politics of Whitehall is often invaluable to groups wishing to understand the corridors of power. As we shall see later there have been concerns about the propriety of former ministers and civil servants working for organisations that lobby government, such as pressure groups, business organisations and lobbying companies. These are discussed in the next chapter.

Alliances with other groups

Pressure groups rarely act in isolation. Most groups realise that in order to influence policy they have to join together with other groups. There are a number of benefits from such alliances. Resources can be pooled. Duplication of effort can be minimised. Moreover, each participant can use its particular strengths to enhance the alliance as a whole. For example some groups may have a high public profile and good media contacts. Others may have good communications with Whitehall departments or with MPs. Furthermore, an effective alliance of groups is in some ways greater than the some of its parts. Indeed a coalition of diverse groups all calling for the same thing represents a formidable lobby and one which has to be taken seriously by government. Such advantages creates strong incentives for groups to work together and results in some unusual alliances. For examples, the lobby opposing the repeal of Section 28 of the Local Government Act 1988, which prohibits local authorities from intentionally promoting homosexuality, included a wide range of religious organisations including the Church of England and the Catholic Church along with organisations representing the

Muslim, Hindu, Sikh and Jewish faiths. Another example is the cooperation between the rival motoring organisations, the AA and the RAC, on issues of mutual concern such as road safety. There are of course disadvantages and costs of forming alliances. Groups have to create coordinating mechanisms which can be bureaucratic. Individual groups may have to compromise on some issues in order to pursue a common goal, which could cause internal problems for them if their members and supporters are opposed to such a move.

There are several different types of alliance. At a basic level groups may agree to keep their allies informed of their lobbying efforts. Alternatively, they may co-operate further by jointly lobbying decision-makers. A higher level of co-operation is the creation of joint committees to coordinate activity. An example of this is the joint committee established by the RSPCA and the RSPB to consider the problems of international trade in rare birds. Groups may also decide to create a new group as an umbrella organisation to act in their joint interests. An example is the Long Term Medical Conditions Alliance (LMCA) which includes over a hundred patients' and carer organisations and which seeks to represent the interests of chronically ill people and those who care for them. The most ambitious form of umbrella group is the 'peak association' which organises interests within a particular sector. Examples include the Trades Union Congress and the Confederation of British Industry. Peak associations can be very influential because of there sheer size and financial resources. However, because of their large affiliated memberships and their diversity of interests they are prone to internal tensions over priorities and tactics and can find it difficult to adopt a coherent position on some policy issues.

Finally, it should be noted that alliances can occur at different levels in the political system. Groups can come together at local level, as illustrated by the anti-roads protestors for example. They may form alliances at national level for the purpose of shaping central government policy, or (as has already been illustrated in the context of the European Union – see Exhibit four) they may ally at an international level to lobby European institutions or global bodies such as the United Nations and its agencies.

Economic factors

Economic factors enter into pressure group politics in two main ways. First of all, above a very basic level of activity, pressure groups require economic resources to mount campaigns. Offices in London (and increasingly, Brussels too) are costly to maintain. The employment of permanent staff is also expensive. In addition the actual business of lobbying can incur large bills. Very few groups can afford to wine and dine MPs, hire parliamentary consultants or lobbying companies (see below), or to fund a media campaign. Yet even the more mundane activities such as the production of pamphlets, fact sheets, reports, or the organisation of a protest rally, are not costless. Pressure groups have to get their resources from somewhere.

For some groups raising the necessary financial resources is not a problem. Businesses can finance lobbying out of their profits. Industries such as agriculture, food, alcoholic drink, motor vehicles, tobacco, defence equipment, oil, chemicals and pharmaceuticals, not to mention the financial and retail sectors, spend a vast amount of money on political campaigns to persuade government to adopt policies which enhance or at least maintain their profitability. For example, the tobacco industry has since the 1960s campaigned vigorously against a ban on advertising and sponsorship (see exhibit four) .

Trades associations and trade unions have a ready source of finance in the form of subscriptions from their members. Some consumer groups are also funded by subscriptions, including the Consumers' Association. Some cause groups also have a mass membership (such as the Royal Society for the Protection of Birds which astonishingly has around a million members) which can generate a substantial income, some of which may be used for campaigning.

As noted earlier, some pressure groups, particularly voluntary organisations which provide services, receive grants from central or local government agencies. But most rely on public donations to fund their campaigns. The larger charities generate huge incomes from the public. The RSPCA for example raised £27m from the public in 1991. However, the less well-known causes have great difficulty in raising money from public donations. One should note here that charity law imposes restrictions on the ability of registered charities to undertake political campaigns. In particular any activity likely to be construed as 'party political' is prohibited. But charities must be able to demonstrate that any political activities they undertake are both ancillary to and directly in support of their objectives, that benefit to the public must be paramount, and that 'there is a reasonable expectation that the activity concerned will further the stated purposes of the charity, and so benefit its beneficiaries, to an extent justified by the resources devoted to the activity' [2]. This latter provision is important because it means in affect that charities have to be careful that the expenditure on lobbying campaigns does not exceed what might be viewed by others as an unreasonable amount. The constraints imposed by the above are not theoretical, in the past high profile charities such as Oxfam and War on Want have been subject to inquiries by the Charity Commission with regard to their campaigning activities.

Aside from the resourcing of political activity, economic factors are important in another sense. If a pressure group speaks for an interest that is economically significant, it will tend to get a sympathetic hearing. Business and industrial organisations are in this position because they are a source of national prosperity, jobs, tax revenues and export earnings. However not all industrial interests are equally powerful. The oil industry is regarded as far more powerful than fishing industry, for example. The financial sector is generally regarded as having more political clout than manufacturing sector. When such interests conflict it is possible to see which is the stronger. It was often claimed that in the 1980s, financial sector appeared to have much more influence over economic policy than manufacturing industry. This was reflected in government policies on interest rates during this period, which remained too high from the point of view of manufacturers, but enabled the financial sector to make huge profits on lending.

Today, it is generally agreed that pressure groups which represent business have greater economic leverage than those representing the workforce. Trade unions have declined as a political force since the 1970s, when the unions were a major economic player. In the era of full employment they exerted a lot of influence over labour markets, wages, and productivity and therefore had a major influence on the economy. The use of the strike weapon in industrial disputes had an impact on the economy as a whole. Moreover, the government also depended upon the unions to help implement key economic policies, such as incomes policies, for example.

The power of trade unions to disrupt production through industrial action was restricted by legislation during the 1980s and 1990s by the Thatcher and Major governments. In addition the economic power of the unions was further undermined by other factors affecting the labour market in this period. In particular, the growth of mass unemployment, the replacement of labour with new technologies, and the increasing use of casual and non-unionised labour in the growing service-based industries weakened the unions' ability to control labour inputs.

Social factors

Many groups which do not have economic power make up for this with what could be called social leverage. Social leverage is the ability of a pressure group to call on support from the public as a whole, or from significant sections of it. Some pressure groups are able to draw on such support because of the social status and prestige of their members. For example, professional bodies and associations, such as the Royal Colleges of Medicine and the BMA, can trade on the public's respect for the profession, which remains high despite media coverage of incompetent and dangerous doctors. For example in a public opinion poll reported in *The Guardian* in January 2000 doctors were given a rating of 8.4 out of 10 for public respect. Nurses came top with 8.5, while at the bottom end estate agents received 3.9, solicitors 5.7, and MPs 5.5 [3].

Meanwhile some groups exert social leverage partly because they are clearly representative of a particular section of society. The BMA is again a good example of this, as it represents 80% of doctors. The National Farmers Union provides another example. It represents 75% of farmers, and is recognised as the main voice of farming.

The overall size of a group's membership is also an indicator of its social leverage. Some groups have huge memberships, such as the National Trust (almost two million members), the Consumers' Association (over one million members). Three trade unions, the Transport and General Workers (TGWU), the Amalgamated Engineering and Electrical Union (AEEU), and the public sector union UNISON, have over a million members each.

Changes in the size of group membership implies changes in the social leverage of groups. For example, trade union membership which stands at 7 million today has declined markedly since the late seventies (when there were over 12 million trade union members in the UK), both in absolute terms and as a proportion of the total workforce. This trend has paralleled the declining influence of the unions. Over the same period the ranks of the environmental lobby have swollen, reflecting the increase in its influence. In 1998 over 5m people were members of environmental groups, though some of these may have joined more than one group [4].

The overall size of a pressure group's membership is important. But if they are to be mobilised, it is crucial that the members have more than a passing commitment to the groups's aims. Some of the mass membership groups have a large proportion of passive members who are difficult to mobilise. For example, most of the members of the Consumers Association join not for political reasons but to obtain the other benefits of membership, such as the consumer magazine *Which?*.

The intensity of feeling among the group's membership is perhaps the key factor. A numerically small group but intense group can exert more influence than a larger, less committed one. One finds that such groups are able to block or delay decisions, even when there is a majority in favour of change. Water fluoridation is a case in point. In the past schemes to add fluoride to water have been backed by a majority of the public and by dentists and medical professionals who believe that this intervention will improve dental health. But schemes have been thwarted by small, well-organised groups concerned about the health effects of fluoridation and the lack of individual choice which results from fluoridation. Similarly a small, well-organised minority can take advantage of public passivity to change the law. A good example of this was 'Passport for Pets', a campaign led by Lady Fretwell and a few well-connected individuals who were opposed to quarantine controls for pets. The group was able to persuade the government, the main veterinary bodies, public health experts and animal welfare charities that the rules should be changed. As a result the Pet Travel Scheme was introduced whereby pets would be able to travel more freely with their owners (see Exhibit five).

Exhibit five
The pet travel scheme

This is an interesting case which illustrates how a small minority was able to promote a change in the law. Quarantine controls for animals are widely accepted as a means of protecting the public from diseases, such as rabies which is endemic in some parts of the world. However, those who travel regularly or who work overseas can be inconvenienced by these regulations. Until recently pets, such as cats and dogs, had to spend 6 months in quarantine on their return to the UK at an average cost of £1600. This enforced separation was not only expensive but upsetting for pets and their owners.

Support for a change in the rules came from those serving in the armed forces who had been or were likely to be posted overseas. It was also endorsed by wealthy individuals who spent considerable time in other countries on long holidays or who perhaps had second homes there. Government representatives and officials, such as ambassadors and diplomats, were also supportive of change. Indeed the campaign to change the law was spearheaded by Lady Mary Fretwell, the wife of a diplomat. The campaign, Passports for Pets, was established in 1994 to exempt cats and dogs from the quarantine regulations by promoting an alternative scheme whereby animals would be thoroughly checked for diseases and then given identification certificates. It was supported by MPs such as Robert Key (whose constituency of Salisbury interestingly has one of the highest concentrations of armed service personnel in the country). Other MPs interested in the issue including David Amess, Ann Widdecombe, Alan Meale, Roger Gale, Colin Pickthall and the late Alan Clark also supported the campaign as did Chris Patten the former governor of Hong Kong, whose two dogs had to be placed in quarantine when they arrived back in the UK. The press also took on interest, to an extent because some newspaper proprietors were inconvenienced by the present rules and wanted to take their pets on holiday with them.

Passport for Pets did much to persuade the government to remove the existing rules. It also was able to reassure the public that the changes would not expose the UK to diseases such as rabies. It also did much to persuade other key groups to support the changes. The RSPCA was initially opposed to change, but came round to support reform. The main veterinary bodies, the British Veterinary Association and the Royal College of Veterinary Surgeons also endorsed change as did the BMA, the Kennel Club, and the main travel companies. The only significant group opposed to change was the Quarantine Association representing the businesses that provided boarding services for pets in quarantine which would be likely to lose out financially.

Other factors were also important. The House of Commons' Select Committee on Agriculture published a report in 1994 which recommended a change to the quarantine rules for pets. The

Conservative Government refused to adopt this, but the idea did not go away. The campaign was endorsed by the All Party group of MPs on animal welfare which maintained the pressure on government. MPs tried to introduce their own legislation: David Amess introduced a bill in 1997 which though not successful did facilitate a debate on these issue. Ministers were persuaded to establish a scientific advisory committee on the issue (the Kennedy Committee) which in 1998 recommended an alternative system to quarantine for pets. Following this the Blair government consulted on the possibility of change, and almost nine out of ten responses were positive. A Parliamentary debate was then held, most contributions supporting of change. In 1999 the government introduced new regulations in the form of the Pet Travel Scheme: Pilot Arrangements Order 1999. This enabled the introduction of a pilot scheme for England which came into force in February 2000.

Small, intense groups are often active at a local level, attempting to prevent developments which they believe affect their local community in an adverse way. This is not a new phenomenon. In the seventies, for example, the decision to site the third London Airport at Cublington in Buckinghamshire was famously defeated by WARA, the Wing Airport Resistance Association. However, the number of NIMBY (Not In My Back Yard) groups has apparently grown in recent years, partly in view of the growth of the environmental and conservation movements.

Some have scored notable victories. For example, in the 1980s and 1990s the Druridge Bay campaign successfully defeated two threats: the siting of a nuclear power station and the environmental consequences of sand extraction (see Exhibit six). This case illustrates what people can achieve even when faced with powerful interests.

Exhibit six
The Druridge Bay campaign

This case illustrates how a local community group in Northumbria was able to oppose not one but two major developments over a twenty year period. The focus of their protest was a six mile long stretch of coastline known as Druridge Bay. The first of threat began in 1978 when the site was identified as a possible location for a nuclear power station. The Druridge Bay Association comprising mainly local people living in the vicinity of the bay, was formed in 1979 to oppose such a development. Although this group did much to promote public opposition in the region, the campaign seemed to lose momentum. In particular it proved difficult to coordinate the diverse organisations which had a potential stake in the issue, such as civic groups, local authorities, environmental groups, trade unions, anti-nuclear groups, and conservation groups. The selection of Druridge Bay as one of six possible sites for development, coupled with the formation of a local branch of Friends of the Earth and the activity of nuclear campaigners within the local trade union movement, improved coordination and led in 1984 to the formation of the Druridge Bay Campaign, which consisted of 38 organisations and 500 individuals. The organisation had two part-time staff and an office.

The DBC was extremely active in mobilising local opinion through public rallies and other events. The local media were highly supportive and gave plenty of coverage to the protestors' case. All the local Labour and Liberal MPs were persuaded to back the campaign. Of the three Conservative MPs, only one opposed the siting of the power station at Druridge, though remaining committed to nuclear power in principle. All the local authorities in the area were also persuaded to fight the plans. The strong feeling locally was made clear to the government, both directly and in Parliament and in the media. Meanwhile, the Chernobyl disaster strengthened the hand of all the communities who faced a nuclear power station being built in their midst. Furthermore the Thatcher Government's decision to privatise the electricity industry put nuclear power under greater scrutiny. The DBC along with other local groups and national organisations opposed to nuclear power pressured MPs to raise questions about the efficiency and safety of nuclear power generally. In the event the nuclear power stations were withdrawn from the privatisation programme (though the newer power stations were sold off in 1996). In 1994 a moratorium was placed on nuclear power stations in the public sector and the significantly the land purchased at Druridge Bay remained in public hands. Eventually, Magnox Electric, the public sector body which now owned the land, agreed to sell the land for agricultural or residential use.

The DBC also took on Ready Mixed Concrete, whose subsidiary worked under a long lease to extract sand at Druridge Bay. The DBC believed that excessive amounts of sand were being extracted and that this was related to coastal erosion as well as being disruptive to local wildlife, to those who wished to use the bay as an amenity and to people living on the main access routes to the bay. A public campaign was launched, and as with the nuclear campaign people were invited to events at the Bay to show their support. Meanwhile, local authorities and local MPs agreed to endorse the cause. The issue was raised in Parliament and with the Department of the Environment. This pressure culminated in Ready Mixed Concrete's decision to cease its activities at the Bay, 56 years earlier than legally it need have done so. *Sources:* [5]

Finally, pressure groups exert social leverage by mobilising a much broader and deeper kind of support from the wider community. Professional groups, such as doctors and nurses, can generate public support on the basis of the general respect for their work. Other groups may win support because the plight of their members has attracted the sympathy of the public. An example is the Gulf War veterans' fight for compensation relating to Gulf War Syndrome. Another was the Snowdrop campaign. Following the tragedy at Dunblane in March 1996, where 16 children and their teacher were killed by a gunman, a campaign was launched to ban the private ownership of handguns. The group, which drew on the support of the bereaved parents, conducted a high profile campaign which attracted widespread public sympathy. Its efforts resulted in a handgun ban, despite the protests of the gun lobby.

Most cause groups are actively involved in trying to win over the hearts of the public. If successful they can use this support as a resource with which to promote action by government. Pressure groups which represent a particular client group, such as Shelter (the housing and homelessness campaign), the Child Poverty Action Group, Age Concern, are often able to attract public support by demonstrating the respective plight of the homeless, the poor, and the elderly. For some groups, however, this task is not easy. If the client group is one which does not readily attract public sympathy (prisoners, for example) the group will face an uphill struggle. Also in many cases groups face an adversary which is competing for the sympathy of the public, which makes it more difficult to mobilise public support. For example, the pro-abortion lobby's efforts are negated to some extent by the pro-life campaigners. The battle for public support and the social leverage this brings is obviously easier in the absence of another group campaigning for an opposing viewpoint.

Sanctions, direct action and protest

Pressure groups may be in a position where they can inflict damage on the government by resorting to sanctions. In some situations merely the implicit threat of sanctions may persuade the policymakers to listen to their arguments. Sanctions therefore can be seen as a resource, the possession of which may increase influence. Sanctions take a variety of forms. Economic sanctions, such as the withdrawal of investment by multinational corporations, or industrial action by trade unions is an aspect of economic leverage has already been discussed. Other sanctions include consumer boycotts, such those directed against South Africa by anti-apartheid campaigners from the 1960s until the regime fell. Another sanction is to refuse to co-operate with the implementation of government policy. Pressure groups may be able to win concessions by refusing to cooperate with the government policy. The teachers unions for example forced a review of the government's policy on assessment during the early 1990s by refusing to cooperate with pupil testing. The poll tax non-payment campaign of the 1980s, promoted by the Anti Poll Tax Federation, represents a further example. This campaign undoubtedly added to the costs of the tax, in particular by raising collection costs. It also provided a focal point for wide public discontent about the tax, which ultimately led to its abolition.

The effectiveness of sanctions depends on the nature of the issue, in particular how the sanction will affect key policies and economic indicators. Sanctions can be a rather crude weapon. In some cases the government may call campaigners' bluff . Moroever, pressure groups which have enjoyed a close relationship with government will be reluctant to jeopardise a good relationship with ministers and civil servants by making such threats.

In order to be effective, such activities have to affect policy in a significant way. They also require a great deal of public support. The sanctions adopted both by the teachers and by the anti-poll tax campaign seriously undermined key policies and were based on a groundswell of public opposition to these policies.

Sanctions can be regarded as a type of direct action. Although they may well be used as a bargaining counter (as in the case of the teaching unions) this is not always so (as in the case of the poll tax campaign). Direct action, however, covers a broader range of activity, legal and illegal, where pressure groups seek to undermine policy decisions by taking action at a grass roots level. For example, the activities of the radical wing of the animal welfare lobby indulges in a range of activities such as breaking into laboratories and releasing animals used in experiments.

More often though direct action is undertaken to influence rather than bypass the conventional policy process. Most forms of direct action seek to bring facts to public attention (for example the cruelty to animals involved in experiments), or to act as a focus for protest (for example, mass trespass,

The 1980s and 1990s were host to what some believed was a new type of politics. Rather than operate through what could be termed the conventional political channels many campaigns used the techniques of protest politics to make their case. Examples included anti-roads protestors, campaigns against nuclear power and nuclear weapons, animal exports, animal welfare more generally, Genetically Modified (GM) food and environmental pollution. But some have questioned the distinctiveness of modern protest politics. After all many of the direct action techniques adopted by contemporary activists mirror those undertaken many years ago by groups such as the suffragettes for example. There is also little concrete evidence that the public was more willing to engage in protest during the 1990s compared with say the 1970s or 1980s. Although there is evidence of a slight increase in the public's approval or tolerance of protest activity, there is nothing to suggest that individuals are actually more likely to participate in such activities themselves. There is an indication that the public is more assertive, more willing to respond if faced with a decision which they believe to be unjust, but this does not necessarily translate into an increase in protest group activity.

The extent to which protest groups seek to bypass 'conventional' political systems is also questionable. Some of the most prominent protest campaigns of the 1990s, such as Brent Spar or the Snowdrop Campaign example, were orchestrated in such a way as to place public pressure on decision-makers [6]. But in so doing the groups had at some point to engage the conventional political system, by operating through the media and /or Parliamentary pressure. Indeed a group that relies wholly on protest will rarely be successful.

marches, sit ins and so on). The latter was very much in evidence during the late 1990s when a number of cities were brought to a standstill by lorry drivers whose blocked roads to protest about the levels of fuel duty. Another example was the Brent Spar incident of 1995 where Greenpeace occupied an oil storage buoy which was to be disposed at sea by its owners Shell UK. Clever news management by the environmentalists made this a key issue, with the result that Shell (and the UK government which had endorsed its plans) had to make an embarrassing climbdown [7]. The reporting of such tactics by the media to a large extent determines the impact of direct action. As Grant Jordan has written 'protest without media coverage is like a mime performance in the dark: possible but fairly pointless' [8]. The role of the media in relation to pressure group politics and the policy process is discussed further in the next chapter.

CONCLUSION

Pressure groups have a wide range of resources. Indeed there can be few groups that do not have any resources at all, though it does appear that some are relatively well endowed in a number of resource areas. For example, the BMA has professional status, public respect, a large membership, expertise, considerable resources and it is the main representative group in the sector. It is difficult to determine which resources are the most important, since one is not comparing like with like. Generally economic leverage is seen as the most important but much depends on the nature of the issue. Public support in some circumstances can outweigh economic leverage. Much therefore depends on circumstances and the wider political environment (see chapter six). But a great deal also depends on how political resources are utilised in building and maintaining political contacts, which the subject of the next chapter.

Pressure group contacts

INTRODUCTION

With the exception of some forms of direct action, such as boycotts for example, pressure group resources are of little value unless they can be channeled into the political process. In other words pressure groups require good contacts with the main centres of agenda-setting and decision making. These 'pressure points' have already been outlined in an earlier chapter. In this section we take this a stage further by looking more precisely at how pressure groups use these political channels.

ASK YOURSELF

- Which political contacts are the most effective and why?
- Why might pressure groups target specific pressure points?
- What rules should govern the relationships between pressure groups and decision-makers?

MAIN TEXT

Executive contact

Meetings with ministers, their advisers, and senior civil servants is generally regarded as a highly influential channel of influence. Access to senior decision makers is restricted, and is often seen as a privileged status by those facing difficulties of access. This is implicit in Wyn Grant's distinction between insiders and outsiders, discussed in an earlier chapter. However, to be consulted is not necessarily to be influential. Groups may gain privileged access but may not always get their way.

Consultation takes a variety of forms. Much is institutionalised in the form of Whitehall committees. These advise government on policy issues within a defined area of responsibility. The membership of such committees is usually drawn from experts in the field or representatives of groups which have specialised knowledge of the policy area. For example the Standing Medical Advisory Committee (SMAC), which advises the Secretary of State for Health on medical issues, contains representatives from the BMA and Royal Colleges of Medicine. Another example is the Standing Advisory Committee on Trunk Road Assessment which advises the Department of Environment Transport and Regions, This committee contains a range of stakeholders, including members drawn from Transport 2000 and the CBI, as well as academic experts in transport policy

There are literally hundreds of advisory committees in Whitehall. At the latest count there were 544 advisory committees, though this figure excludes most ad hoc working groups and task forces (see below) established by departments. Some advisory committees explore extremely detailed issues, particularly where the government requires specialist knowledge. For example, the Advisory Committee on the Microbiological Safety of Food, advises the government on the prevention of food poisoning. The membership of this committee is drawn from science, medicine, and the food industry. Environmental health officers and consumers are also represented on the committee.

Governments can also set up Committees of Inquiry to investigate pressing issues, which again can provide a focus for groups to put their case. An example is the Committee of Inquiry set up in 1999 to consider the issue of a ban on hunting with dogs. Recently though these have tended to give way to ad hoc 'task forces'. Many task forces have been established in recent years on a wide range of issues; in all 38 were established between May 1997 and October 1999 [1]. Examples include the task force chaired by Lord Rogers on Urban Regeneration, the task force on the government's New Deal Programme, chaired by Peter Davis the Chief Executive of Prudential PLC, the Numeracy Task Force headed by Professor David Reynolds and the Football Task Force chaired by the former Conservative MP, David Mellor.

Various groups are represented on these task forces. Indeed there has been much concern that business groups are over-represented at the expense of others. One report found that half the members of task forces set up after the 1997 General election were drawn from the business sector. 12 companies were represented on three or more task forces. [2]. It has also been alleged that professional lobbyists (which are discussed later in this chapter) have been used to ensure that certain companies are represented on task forces [3]. Another concern is that the task forces have varied in their approach to openness. Some such as the Football Task Force have been very open, encouraging comments from the public through open meetings for example. Others have been very secretive, and as Platt [4] has noted, 'hardly any hold public discussions'

On issues of major concern governments have established public inquiries and Royal Commissions to gather views. Groups and individuals give evidence to these bodies, which produce a report on the issue in question making recommendations. A recent example is the Royal Commission on Long Term Care which reported in 1999. There have been fewer Royal Commissions during the 1980s and 1990s compared with the preceding decades. Indeed during the Thatcher era, no new Royal Commissions were appointed. These bodies have certain advantages: they can build consensus by developing proposals that attract public and cross party support, they can give authority to certain policy options. On the other hand they can be seen as ways of getting issues off the political agenda, at least temporarily. They are also relatively expensive way of examining problems and developing policies. It should be noted that some Royal Commissions on ongoing; they are not dissolved when they have completed their report. Perhaps the most prominent example is the Royal Commission on Environmental Pollution, established in 1970, which has an ongoing brief to advise on matters concerning pollution, the adequacy of research in this field, and future threats to the environment.

Government departments also seek comments on policy proposals from pressure groups on a routine basis. For this purpose they set up panels, forums or reference groups to consult organisations. For example, following protests from the road haulage industry on a variety of issues including vehicle taxation, ministers established a forum to discuss these matters. Similarly, the government has created reference groups to assist its review of health policy issues such as mental health and heart disease. These reference groups contained health professionals, representatives of NHS organisations, charities and patients' organisations.

In addition to these structures, all government departments maintain consultation lists. Groups listed receive consultation papers which outline a policy problem or new proposals for change, and are asked to comment by a certain date. Some of these consultation papers are more specific and detailed than others. Some also have a higher profile than others. Those with the highest profile are usually called Green Papers and these involve much more in the way of public consultation. The first Green Paper was issued in 1967 on the subject of regional policy. Green Papers are usually issued on subjects where the government has not made up its mind on policy or where it is reluctant to state its position. These are meant to contrast with White Papers, where the government sets out its main policy proposals. An example was the Blair Government's Green Paper on Public Health, *Our Healthier Nation*, which set out the government's ideas for improving the health of the public by for example reducing deaths from cancer, heart disease, mental illness and accidents [5]. Hundreds of individuals and organisations responded to this document which was followed up in 1999 with a White Paper *Saving Lives*, which set out the government's policy proposals [6].

However, the difference between Green and White Papers has become rather blurred over the years. During the 1980s Green Papers became much more 'assured ' in their tone, in most cases reflecting the government's position much more clearly. This was partly a reflection of the Thatcher government's style, the wider impact of which will be discussed in a later section.

The methods of consultation discussed so far are rather formal. But the government often solicits views in a less formal manner. Ministers, political advisors and senior civil servants often discuss policy matters informally over lunch with senior members of the professions, top business people, or with the heads of charities and voluntary bodies. They also have informal networks which include pressure group leaders.

The consultation process is extremely important. It provides a means by which government can involve those affected by or having an interest in a policy issue. Indeed, in some cases there is a statutory requirement that government consults certain representative bodies. For example the 1947 Agriculture Act stated that when holding reviews on the state of agriculture 'the ministers shall consult with such bodies of persons as appear to them to represent the interests of producers in the agricultural industry'. More recently the Pollution Prevention and Control Act of 1999 states that before making certain regulations the Secretary of State shall consult 'such bodies or persons appearing to him to be representative of the interests of local government, industry, agriculture, and small businesses respectively as he may consider appropriate'. But this does not mean that consultation should he only be undertaken when the law requires it nor that it should be confined to specific groups. Indeed it is believed by some that open consultation is good practice because it incorporates a wider range of views, builds support for policy initiatives, helps to identify and correct shortcomings in the policy proposals, and leads to better implementation of policies. As hinted at earlier, governments have adopted different approaches to the management of the consultation process and this is also discussed in a later chapter.

The amount of contact between pressure groups and government organisations is extensive and operates at a number of levels. While senior personnel are no doubt important political contacts, one should not ignore the role of middle ranking civil servants. These individuals undertake most of the day to day work on policy issues and are extremely knowledgeable both about the detailed nature of the issues they deal with and the Whitehall machine. They also brief their superiors on policy issues and this can be influential particularly on issues which are relatively uncontroversial, or which are highly technical or have a low public profile. Finally, they are regularly in contact with outside organisations, and are often the first point of contact for a pressure group. A survey undertaken in 1991 found that two thirds of those groups which responded met civil servants at the rank of principal and assistant secretary at least once a month. The groups in the survey on average had slightly more contact with these grades than with MPs and considerably more contact than with higher civil service grades and ministers [7].

There are two main reasons why contacts at this level are so extensive. First of all, most pressure groups will find it difficult to maintain continuous contact with senior policy makers such as ministers and the top grades of the civil service who are dealing with a much wider range of issues. Secondly, such regular contact at this level is not always necessary. Pressure groups often prefer to build up a good working relationship with middle-ranking civil servants who tend to be more knowledgeable about policy details than their superiors.

When groups are dealing with the executive, information about how Whitehall works is extremely useful. For this reason most large pressure groups employ former civil servants. By doing so these groups are not necessarily trying to buy official information or even, for that matter, access to their former colleagues. But they are in effect hiring an insider's technical knowledge about procedures and the way in which Whitehall operates.

Every year a large number of civil servants leave their posts to work for private organisations. For example, in 1991 Mrs Thatcher's former press secretary Sir Bernard Ingham, who was a career civil servant, subsequently became an advisor to British Nuclear Fuels Limited (BNFL). Another example was Sir Duncan Nichol the former chief executive of the NHS, who joined the board of the private health organisation BUPA in 1994 after leaving the service. In 1998 Sir Charles Masefield, the former head of the Defence Export Services at the Ministry of Defence joined GEC, a corporation which is a major defence contractor. Earlier Field Marshall Sir Peter Inge, the former chief of Defence Staff took up a non-executive post with Racal Electronics and became an advisor to Vickers, both of which are involved in the defence industry.

It should be noted that former civil servants do have to abide by certain rules when taking up outside appointments. Senior officials (Permanent Secretary, Deputy Secretary, Under Secretary) require permission within two years of leaving the civil service. The highest ranking civil servants, Permanent Secretaries, must wait a minimum of three months before taking outside employment, although this can be waived. Contentious cases are vetted by the Advisory Committee on Business Appointments, which reports to the Prime Minister. In some cases civil servants can be made to wait for longer periods. For example Sir Peter Inge, mentioned above, had to wait six months rather than the usual three before taking up his post. The Advisory Committee on Business Appointments can also set other conditions relating to civil servants' new employment. For example, they can require that they do not involve themselves in certain types of work relating to their former posts. Less senior civil servants who have had access to commercially sensitive information or who have had close links with an outside organisation during their civil service career are also vetted before being allowed to take up outside appointments. They too can be subject to certain conditions with regard to the length of time that must elapse before they can take a new post and may face restrictions on the nature of the tasks they are allowed to undertake with their new employer. Restrictions may also be imposed on future dealings with their former colleagues in government.

In July 1998 a new code of practice was introduced for civil servants (including ministers' political advisors who are not career civil servants) This included a prohibition on helping professional lobbyists secure privileged access to government. The code also stated that civil servants should consider seeking to balance arguments by eliciting the views of 'opposing groups' when lobbied on a particular issue. The new code stemmed partly from concerns about 'sleaze' during the early 1990s and the subsequent enquiry by the Nolan Committee. Additional allegations about the role of lobbyists and the conduct of political advisors in the Blair Government added weight to the case for strengthening the rules (see Exhibit eight)

Another factor affecting the mobility of personnel between pressure groups and government is secondment. Over the last few two decades government has encouraged the secondment of civil servants to outside organisations and vice versa. Hundreds of secondments in and out of government take place every year. Essentially the idea is to make the civil service less insular: to expose it to fresh ideas and approaches. However, it should be noted that during the Thatcher period most inward secondments (around two thirds) were from business organisations. There is little evidence on what has happened since, though the suspicion that business organisations predominate remains. It should also be noted that in 1995 senior posts in the civil service were opened up to competition with the result that around a third are now filled by applicants from the private sector [8].

Standard civil service rules (see above) cover permanent appointments. Staff on secondment are also expected to operate within the rules on business appointments, though they are exempt if the rejoin their original employer and remain their for at least two years.. But this does not prevent such individuals from using their knowledge of government to the advantage of their original employers. There has also been criticism of the way in which ministers' political advisors have been exempt from the rules of conduct which apply to civil servants. However, since 1996 the appointment rules referred to above have applied to ministerial advisors as well, unless, as with secondments, they rejoin their original employer.

In addition to the concern about the use of former civil servants by outside organisations, there have also been worries about the extent to which former ministers are willing to take up appointments after leaving office. Although ministers must relinquish outside interests when appointed, until fairly recently there was little to stop them from taking up posts with business or other pressure groups when they left office. For example in 1987 Norman Tebbit, who as a former Trade and Industry minister had the task of privatising British Telecom, joined the company as a non-executive director. Similarly Peter Walker, the former Energy minister responsible for privatising the gas industry later took up a post with British Gas. While there is no suggestion of any impropriety in the taking of these jobs, many believe that it is important that former ministers should be subjected to restrictions on their future employment in order to avoid any such allegations being made. Following the Nolan Report (see exhibit eight), the government agreed to implement new system for vetting ex-minister's appointments. This is along similar lines to the procedure for senior civil servants. Ministers must submit to the judgement of the Advisory Committee on Business Appointments which can advise that ministers do not take appointments for up to two years and may impose restrictions on the activities on ex-ministers working for a new employer. This procedure has not prevented former ministers from taking up new posts. Examples include former Chancellor of the Exchequer Kenneth Clarke who is the deputy chairman of British American Tobacco PLC and a non-executive chairman of Unichem PLC. Virginia Bottomley, formerly Secretary of State for Health was an advisor to Wyeth, a drugs company. John Gummer, who served as Secretary of State for the Environment and as the Minister of Agriculture, has among his portfolio a directorship of General Utilities, a company involved in waste and waste management.

By employing former ministers and civil servants, groups can acquire greater knowledge about the workings of central government. This can give them a certain advantage over other groups that do not have this resource. Obviously business groups are in better position to employ former ministers and civil servants, given their financial resources. But other less wealthy groups can also enlist the support of former ministers by offering them honorary posts with the organisation. For example, Virginia Bottomley is a vice patron of the Carers' National Association. Notably, ex-ministers may take up unpaid appointments in non-commercial organisations without having to refer to the Advisory Committee on Business Appointments.

Exhibit eight
The Nolan Report

Allegations about MPs taking money for asking Parliamentary Questions against a background of public dissatisfaction about standards in public life led to the creation of a Committee on Standards in Public Life in 1994 under the chairmanship of Lord Nolan. The Nolan Committee subsequently set out seven principles of public life: selflessness, integrity, objectivity, accountability, openness, honesty and leadership.

Its report, published in 1995, set out a number of recommendations. These included: a prohibition on MPs working for lobbying companies, an independent Parliamentary Commissioner for Standards, clearer disclosure of MPs' interests in the Register of Members' Interests, a code of conduct for MPs, a system of vetting ex-ministers businesses appointments, a new civil service code. The Committee also maintained that appointments to quasi-governmental bodies should more open and made a number of

recommendations to this effect including the appointment of a Commissioner for Public appointments to monitor, regulate and approve appointments procedures.

Most of Nolan's recommendations were accepted. In some respects changes went further than Nolan recommended. For example, MPs voted to rule out paid advocacy on behalf of an outside interest. But the problems of sleaze did not go away either with the implementation of Nolan's recommendations or with the change of government in 1997. Indeed the Blair Government quickly became embroiled in the Ecclestone affair, where critics argued that the government's policy on tobacco sponsorship had been compromised by the donation to the Labour Party from the vice president of the FIA, the international body representing motor racing (see Exhibit four). There was also a row in 1998 when one former Labour Party activist turned lobbyist, Derek Draper boasted of his links with key decision-makers in the Treasury and Downing Street to journalists

posing as businessmen [9]. In addition there were serious allegations against ministers including Geoffrey Robinson and Peter Mandelson, which led to their resignation from the Cabinet.

Following the retirement of Lord Nolan as chairman of the Committee, his successor Lord Neill continued to examine issues related to the conduct of politicians and civil servants. In a report published in January 2000, the Neill Committee proposed a new code of conduct for ministerial advisors to be policed by the permanent secretaries, and recommended that ministers and civil servants should keep records of contacts with lobbyists. Other recommendations included a new system of complaints for MPs accused of serious misconduct and a suggestion that the appointment of individuals to task forces should be monitored.

Contact with the legislature

Despite the fact that the executive in many respects dominates the policymaking process, Parliament remains an important target for lobbying campaigns. Many groups focus on Parliamentary lobbying because they have no alternative. However, it would be wrong to view Parliament necessarily as a last resort. As mentioned above some groups do not seek a close relationship with the government and for them Parliamentary contacts may be more desirable. Moreover, most insider groups, which already have good contacts with the executive, also seek to build a good relationship with Parliament.

Parliamentary lobbying is extensive. A Study of Parliament Group survey reported in 1990 showed that 75% of groups had regular or frequent contact with MPs, and 66% had given evidence to Select Committees, while 47% had contact with all party groups [10]. It is also widely believed that Parliamentary lobbying increased during the 1980s and the 1990s, though there is little more than anecdotal evidence (mainly from the MPs themselves) to support this. However the survey by Baggott did find that a large proportion of groups claimed to have increased their contact with Parliament during the 1980s. 45 per cent reported increased contact with the Commons and 37 per cent increased contact with the Lords [11].

Why has Parliamentary lobbying remained a popular strategy among pressure groups? After all, one would not have expected this given the weakness of Parliament relative to the Executive. There are a number of possible explanations. On reason could be that some pressure groups overestimate the influence of Parliament. After all, situations in which MPs are able to exercise independent judgement, free from the pressures of the party whips, are rare. Even so, MPs have voted on 'conscience issues' such as the age of consent for homosexual acts, hunting, abortion, embryology research, and capital punishment where party pressures are weaker (but not entirely absent) and where groups arguably have greater scope for influence. Also, MPs from the governing party are willing to express their disapproval of policies by abstaining or even voting against the government. The House of Lords too has opposed governments on many occasions (see below) in recent years. Although rebellions in the Commons and the Lords rarely stop a policy in its tracks or lead to legislation being abandoned, they do sometimes force government to rethink its proposals and propose amendments to its chosen course.

The openness of Parliament is another reason why groups approach it. Because access to Westminster is not as restricted as access to Whitehall, it is not surprising that the former remains an important target for lobbying. Even groups with 'insider status' know that contact with MPs and peers is an important complement to a good relationship with Whitehall. Contact with MPs, either on an individual basis, or collectively in the form of select committees and party backbench committees, is extremely useful as a means of finding out what is going on in the world of politics. Such links are also useful in influencing the political agenda as MPs, Peers and Parliamentary committees can take up ideas raised by pressure groups and give them wider support and credibility.

Having explored the value of Parliamentary contacts, let us now look at how pressure groups establish such contacts. Groups can build contacts with MPs in a number of ways: through constituency links, sponsorship and political consultancies, through economic interests, and through other personal interests.

Pressure groups which represent local interests or interests which are geographically concentrated will tend to build links with MPs in the relevant constituencies. Hence MPs in constituencies affected by the Channel Tunnel rail link have been the natural focal point for local pressure groups concerned about this issue. Industries which are concentrated in a particular area often approach their local MP. For example, Janet Dean is the MP for Burton on Trent, a major centre for the brewing industry.

Constituency interests can often be used by pressure groups wishing to mount a broad Parliamentary campaign. Hospital workers, concerned about aspects of the government's NHS reforms have targeted MPs with a major hospital in their constituency. While the tourism industry has tried to build support among MPs representing the main tourist centres in an attempt to persuade the government to promote the industry. For example, MPs such as Gordon Marsden and Joan Humble (respectively the MPs for Blackpool South and Blackpool North and Fleetwood) will be expected to take an interest in leisure and tourism issues because of the importance of these industries to their constituents.

Pressure groups can build links with MPs by hiring them as political consultants. Businesses, trade associations and some professional associations do this, though the amounts involved vary. Around 80 MPs have political consultancies at present. They include John Butterfill (Bournemouth West) Parliamentary Advisor to the British Venture Capital Association, Eric Clarke, (Midlothian) Parliamentary Advisor to Scottish Coal, Derek Foster (Bishop Auckland) Parliamentary Consultant to 3MUK PLC, Simon Hughes, (North Southwark and Bermondsey) Parliamentary Consultant to the Association of Teachers and Lecturers.

The number of MPs with consultancies has fallen. This is believed to be due in part at least to the change in the rules of the House of Commons in the aftermath of the Nolan Report (see Exhibit eight) which in effect banned paid advocacy. MPs were afraid to hold certain consultancies believing that this opened them up to accusations of impropriety. Where consultancies are held it has to be made clear that the job is to advise the client not to lobby on their behalf.

Other links exist between businesses and MPs. Some MPs are directors of companies (such as John Gummer and Kenneth Clarke, mentioned earlier). Others run family businesses, such as Tim Boswell (Daventry) who is a farmer. Others have declared shareholdings in companies and may have a financial rather than a managerial interest in a particular business.

Some MPs have links with the trade union movement. Traditionally trade unions have sponsored Labour MPs by paying money into their constituency fund. Under what became known as the Hastings Agreement there was no personal financial gain to the MP under this arrangement. In return for this funding the MP kept the union informed on political matters and when necessary undertook campaigns in Parliament on its behalf. The Hastings Agreement has now been largely replaced by a system whereby trade unions give funds centrally to the Labour Party rather than to the constituencies. Some unions still donate small amounts though. For example in the Register of Members' Interests in January 2000, Paul Clark the MP for Gillingham declared that the Amalgamated Engineering and Electrical Union donated £1000 to his constituency party. It should be noted that some MPs have other links with the unions. Some, such as Angela Eagle (Wallasey), Oona King (Bethnal Green and Stepney) and John Prescott (Hull East) were all formerly trade union officials. Some MPs are still members of trade unions, such as David Hinchcliffe, the MP for Wakefield who is a member of Unison.

The extent of MPs' economic interests has prompted worries about their judgement. Concern has been compounded by other developments such as the growth of commercial lobbying companies, to be discussed in a later section. MPs are required to declare their interests when appropriate, such as when taking part in a debate. Since 1975, MPs have been expected to enter pecuniary interests and material benefits in the Register of Members' Interests. Failure to comply with these rules can lead to suspension from the House of Commons. More recently, the rules and procedures have been tightened following the Nolan Report (see Exhibit eight).

MPs can also represent professional interests. For example, Alan Hurst (Braintree) is a lawyer, and a member of the law society. There are also several doctors in the House of Commons, including Dr Roger Stoate (Dartford) who is also a member of the BMA, a regular contributor to debates about health policy and medicine.

Indeed MPs also adopt causes on the basis of principle or for personal reasons. For example Kevin McNamara (Hull North) is a senior member of the League Against Cruel Sports. Virginia Bottomley (SW Surrey) is a vice patron of the Carers' National Association. Beverley Hughes (Stretford and Urmston) is member of Oxfam, Action Aid, and Amnesty International while Alan Simpson (Nottingham South) is a member of CND, Oxfam and Shelter.

Given their wide range of interests, MPs are very open to pressure groups lobbying. Groups will tend to be selective in approaching MPs, confining their lobbying to those who have a particular interest in the issue, those with whom they have worked before, or MPs who they believe are opinion formers on the issue. These MPs can then act as conduits to influence Parliamentary opinion. However, much depends on the nature of the issue. Pressure groups may resort to a direct appeal to MPs, through a mass lobby of Parliament or a mass mailing of MPs. This can be successful in following 'behind the scenes activity' by MPs in Parliament already on the side of the group. However, in isolation this is rarely effective, and is usually seen as a last resort.

MPs can be persuaded to undertake a number of activities in support of the group. These include supporting Early Day Motions (statements of opinion, to which MPs can add their name), Parliamentary Questions, initiating and speaking in debates and introducing Private Members' Bills. All these serve to focus the government's attention on a group's campaign. In some circumstances a group may be successful in promoting a direct change in the law through private member's legislation. But as such legislation requires government support, Parliamentary lobbying alone is unlikely to be sufficient. MPs can be persuaded by groups to amend government legislation. Although in most cases the system of party discipline tends to operate against this, the whips can convey sentiments expressed by backbench MPs back to the government, and this can result in a compromise amendment being introduced by ministers to take the sting out of a potential rebellion by MPs.

Pressure groups not only target individual MPs, they seek to influence Parliamentary committees. These committees can be influential in shaping Parliamentary opinion and can in some situations have an impact on the policy process. Many groups have close relations with All Party Groups (APGs), which as their name suggests draw in MPs from all the political parties. There are over a hundred APGs, examples include the Animal Welfare All Party Committee and the All Party Committee on Smoking and Health. Pressure Groups use these groups to keep MPs informed of their activities and by the same token MPs keep groups abreast of Parliamentary developments. In addition to the APGs, each Parliamentary Party has its own subject groups which cover the whole range of policy issues. These subject groups, particularly those of the governing party, can be useful targets for pressure groups wishing to build support for their case in Parliament.

Select Committees also contain MPs from different parties. These committees monitor government and attempt to hold it to account by investigating its activities. Some committees focus on the work of specific departments or agencies, such as the Health Committee and the Home Affairs Committee. Others cut across departmental boundaries, including the Public Accounts Committee, which examines government expenditure, and the Committee on Public Administration which looks at general issues of management and accountability in the public sector.

The Select Committees make recommendations on the basis of their inquiries. Although they cannot compel government to change its policies, they play a useful role in getting issues on to the agenda and in some cases getting the government to reconsider aspects of its policy where these are shown to be failing. A good example of this is the Social Security Committee's reports on the Child Support Agency which added to the pressure on government to reform the system. Although calls by pressure groups giving evidence to the committee for the Agency to be abolished were not heeded, recommendations made by the committee to improve the system were considered by government.

Select Committees take evidence from pressure groups (as well as individuals and other organisations) when undertaking their inquiries. This provides an ideal opportunity for groups to put across their arguments. If these are endorsed by the Committee this adds considerable weight to group's case. Although, as noted, there is no guarantee that the government will respond positively, this does tend to add momentum to a group's campaign.

Other important committees of the House are the Standing Committees. These consider legislation in detail and obviously attract the attention of groups trying to influence the details of policy. Pressure groups brief MPs on the relevant standing committee and lobby them to introduce or (as the case may be) to block amendments. Under a special Standing Committee procedure it is possible for standing committees to take evidence directly from interested parties. In this way pressure groups can put their case alongside the views of others, enabling the MPs to hear all sides of the argument.

Finally, when looking at the relationship between pressure groups and Parliament one should not forget the House of Lords. In the survey by the Study of Parliament Group, mentioned earlier, 59% of the pressure groups in the survey had regular or frequent contact with the Lords. The survey by Baggott [12] found that half the groups were in touch with peers on at least a monthly basis. The House of Lords has become increasingly useful to pressure groups, particularly those frustrated by their inability to influence a government-dominated House of Commons. For example, between 1979 and 1990 the House of Lords defeated the Conservative government on over 150 occasions. Some of these victories were short-lived, with the government reversing the Lords' amendments when the bills returned to the Commons. But even when this happens, pressure groups often got additional publicity for their case.

Moreover, in many cases the government has often had to rethink its plans in the light of a defeat in the Upper House. This has often produced a compromise, as on one of the clauses in the Education Reform Bill of 1988, when the local authority associations among others lobbied furiously for a change in the rules which enabled schools to opt out of local authority control. Attention focused on the balloting of parents, an important part of the opting out procedure. The Lords defeated the government by inserting a requirement that a majority of all eligible parents would have to vote for opting out in order to proceed. The government compromised by permitting a second ballot where less than half the eligible parents had taken part in the original vote.

When a government has a large majority, it has been more difficult for the Lords to get it to rethink its plans. However, it is not impossible. Even the Blair Government has been forced to compromise on some of its policies. For example in February 2000 the Lords caused government to think again on the repeal of 'clause 28', which prohibits the intentional promotion of homosexuality by local authorities. The government was defeated by 210 votes to 165. A month later revised plans on sex education were also defeated in the Lords. At around the same time, the Blair Government suffered a reversal was again defeated on aspects of its plans to introduce new management arrangements in local councils. In all these cases peers were subjected to extensive lobbying by pressure groups.

It should be noted that changes in composition of the Lords may have an effect on its usefulness as a target for pressure groups. Under the Blair Government's interim plans for the Lords, which came into force in 1999, the right of all but 92 hereditary peers to sit and vote in the House was ended. At the time of going to press, (August 2000) these peers sit alongside 558 life peers and 26 bishops and archbishops. In 1999, a Royal Commission on the House of Lords issued a report calling for a new chamber to be established that would be broadly representative of society. It recommended that a majority should be appointed and that there would also be elected regional members, though the exact number of members was not stipulated. It also called a more balanced ethnic and gender representation and for wider representation of religious faiths in the chamber.

At the time of writing the government's plans have not been clarified. But one or two general observations can be made. First, a substantial proportion of elected members will give the House greater legitimacy and may increase its ability to wring concessions from the government. Secondly, the appointment of individuals may increase the independence of the Lords, particularly if the process of appointment is, as the Royal Commission has suggested, operated by an independent commission. Third, the opportunities of specific pressure groups to make their case may be enhanced if the House is more representative of society. In particular, women's groups, ethnic groups and the regions will probably have more scope to put their case if the Commission's recommendations are followed.

Correspondingly other interests may well lose out as a result of reform. Landed and interests for example will probably have fewer direct representatives. The agricultural and rural voice may also be weakened following changes to the composition of the House. It is also likely that there will be much more concern about the interests of members in the Upper House, post-reform. In 1995 the House of Lords did introduce a register of interests and new rules of conduct. The rules stated that Lords who accept payment or reward for providing Parliamentary services or how who have a financial interest in a lobbying company (see below) should not speak, vote, lobby or take advantage of their position as members. The registration of consultancies and financial interests in lobbying companies was a mandatatory requirement. However, the registration of other financial interests and other links with outside organisations was discretionary. As the profile of the new chamber rises, as seems likely to be the case, it is probable that demands for a tougher system of interest declaration will occur. Indeed at the time of writing the Neill Committee on Standards in Public Life is examining whether the present system should be reformed. A compulsory register with penalties for breaking the rules is one suggestion that is being explored.

Professional lobbyists

Rather than represents their own interests directly, some pressure groups, particularly business organisations and overseas interests, prefer to operate through professional lobbying companies. These provide a range of services for their clients including political briefings, keeping the client informed about the political environment, advice on how to go about influencing policy, and attempting to influence policy on behalf of a client. Lobbying companies can be seen as political middlemen, a bridge between groups and decision makers. They act as facilitators, arranging meetings between their clients and ministers, civil servants, or MPs.

Some companies have an impressive list of clients. For example, Westminster Communications' client list has included Cellnet. Public Policy Consultants have acted for Proctor and Gamble, the Association of District Councils, and Britannia Airways. Another firm, Westminster Strategy has worked on behalf of the Japanese electronics industry, and the Certified Accountants' professional body[13]. Lawson Lucas Mendelsohn's clients have included Anglian Water, News International, and Orange[14].

The growth of lobbying companies has caused concern for a number of reasons. First of all, some believe that the services offered enhance the position of groups, namely those with financial resources which are already powerful relative to others. Secondly, there is concern that some of their activities could undermine the independent judgement of MPs, leading to the dominance of private over public interests.

However, it is difficult to assess the influence of lobbying companies. After all, as commercial organisations they have to boast about their influence in order to attract customers. There is some anecdotal evidence to suggest they can be influential but their successes often occur on technical issues of fairly low political significance. It is unlikely that their activities could be successful in the face of strong public opposition though it should be noted that many of these companies are also active in public relations, and are therefore skilled in manipulating public opinion.

In recent years there has been a great deal of concern about the interaction of professional lobbying organisations and decision-makers, particularly their contact with Parliament. Criticism of the links between lobbying companies and MPs during the 1980s and 1990s led to calls for greater regulation of these relationships. The Nolan Committee recommended a ban on MPs working for lobbying companies. Instead new rules governing 'paid advocacy' were introduced which if enforced should prevent lobbying companies from retaining MPs for the purpose of directly representing the interests of clients in Parliament. However, the new rules do allow MPs to be employed by and to have a financial stake in lobbying companies providing that their role is confined to giving advice. Around the same time the House of Lords also introduced rules governing paid advocacy and made the registration of interests with regard to lobbying companies a mandatory requirement.

Criticism of the activities of lobbying companies has not abated. Indeed it was revealed that some professional lobbyists had established close links with key government personnel. In the Draper case (see Exhibit eight) it was revealed that a professional lobbyist who had previously worked as an advisor to Peter Mandelson (who later became a government minister) had boasted of his contacts within government. Although special advisors were already subject to rules on taking up appointments after leaving government, it was felt that more needed to be done to regulate the relationship between lobbyists and government appointees. In 1999, special advisors (and civil servants) were given additional guidance on how to deal with professional lobbyists (see Exhibit eight). A further suggestion was the introduction of a register of lobbyists such as that found in the United States, Australia and Canada. A registration scheme was backed by the House of Commons Select Committee on Members Interests in 1991 and this was endorsed by most lobbying companies. But the recommendation was not been taken any further, largely because, a register confers a kind of approved status on those who are listed on it and may encourage outside organisations to use them. Notably the Committee on Standards in Public Life in a report of January 2000, rejected calls for a formal register of lobbyists [15].

Links with the media

Public support alone is rarely enough to persuade decision-makers to adopt or reject a particular course of action. However, as mentioned in a previous section, pressure groups often require public support to further their case.

Indeed, high profile public campaigns are seen increasingly as a complementary activity, a valuable aid to negotiations in Whitehall and Parliamentary lobbying.

Even well-established insider groups, such as the BMA and the RSPCA have adopted mass media advertising campaigns in recent years. Such campaigns cost an enormous amount of money and can only be afforded by the wealthiest groups. Because of the prohibitive cost of advertising, many groups tend to rely on the free publicity of news coverage. But attracting the interest of news and current affairs journalists is easier for some groups than others. The media are attracted by powerful or unusual images. The occupation in 1995 by Greenpeace of the Brent Spar storage and loading buoy belonging to Shell UK was a case in point. The 'David and Goliath ' battle at sea between the protestors and the company was attractive to both the press and the broadcast media. This case illustrated how pressure groups, desperate for such coverage, deliberately seek to attract media attention through 'set-piece' events. The campaign group Surfers Against Sewage provides another example. This groups has been very successful in highlighting the pollution of beaches and coastal waters by attracting media attention. To make their point, activists, clad in wetsuits and gas masks, have surfed in sewage-ridden water or floated in brown inflatable dinghies. This spectacle has attracted the attention of the media and even resulted in a television documentary about the issue of sewage pollution which examined the activities of the group.

Often newspapers, television, and radio documentaries and consumer programmes will take up a cause which has been raised in this way. The tabloid press was instrumental in forcing the government to take action against dangerous dogs in the late eighties. Television and radio documentaries also have had a major role in getting issues on to the agenda. Documentary programmes such as 'Dispatches' and 'Panorama' can mobilise public opinion. But even drama can have an impact. Perhaps 'Cathy Come Home', a drama from the 1960s which focused attention on the plight of homeless families, is still the best example. This led to a public outcry, and with the formation of the pressure group Shelter, placed enormous pressure on politicians to do something about the problem.

Consumer programmes such as 'Watchdog' have also fought campaigns on specific issues. In doing so they have often had very close contact with consumer and other pressure groups, and have relied on these groups for information and research. Watchdog has also fought a number of successful campaigns. For example it played a major role in the campaign for new regulations governing the sale of household electrical products. 'Watchdog' raised public awareness about the number of people electrocuted by badly-wired plugs on TVs, kettles and so on. The new regulations aimed to reduce this toll by requiring suppliers to fit plugs, properly wired, to their products before sale.

Publicity is often linked to direct action, as the Brent Spar case illustrated. The anti GM food campaigners for example took steps to disrupt farm trials not only in an effort to prevent further research but to raise public concern. Other groups have also used direct action and mass protests to court publicity. Example include mass trespasses on private land, organised by ramblers to attract support for the 'right to roam'. Protest marches, such as those organised by the Campaign for Nuclear Disarmament and more recently by the Countryside Alliance were also useful in mobilising public sentiment. However, where protests end in disorder this can be counterproductive, as public support tends to be discouraged by scenes of violence. But this is not always the case. The protests against live animal exports and road building schemes during the 1990s gave rise to allegations that protestors had been roughly treated by the police. The fact that some of the alleged victims included elderly people and women attracted some public sympathy for their position. In one incident in 1995 a young woman, Jill Phipps, was crushed to death under a lorry while protesting against animal exports at Coventry airport. This personal tragedy had wider political implications in that it served to focus enormous public attention on the issue and strengthened the resolve of campaigners.

Exhibit nine
GM food protests

The case of genetically modified (GM) foods provides a good example of the politics of pressure. Some GM foods had already been introduced into the UK, such as tomato puree, without much fuss. But environmental groups, such as the Green Party, Greenpeace and Friends of the Earth, conservationists including Royal Society for the Protection of Birds and the government agency English Nature, consumer groups such as the Consumers' Association, health groups including the British Medical Association, and organic farmers all became increasingly concerned about GM foods for a number reasons. First, there were possible implications for human health. Although there was no evidence to suggest that GM food was damaging to human health, the prospect of such an impact in the future could not be guaranteed. Against the background of the 'Mad Cow Disease' crisis and other food issues such as pesticides contamination and the overuse of antibiotics, these fears could not easily be dismissed. Secondly, there was concern about the lack of consumer choice and information. The labelling of GM foods was very limited. New measures were subsequently introduced by the European Union and by the UK, though failed to satisfy many critics. Moreover, because US suppliers did not distinguish GM soya and maize from non-GM produce, food manufacturers and retailers could not label these products as 'GM free' in order that consumers could if they wished avoid them. Third, there was concern about implications for wildlife and their habitats. Environmentalists and conservationists were worried that commercial growing of GM crops could

have a catastrophic effect on insects and birds and on the diversity of plant life. English Nature, a government agency, asked the government for a three year moratorium on commercial growth of GM crops resistant to herbicides until far, trials were completed. Fourth, there was concern about organic farming and the uncontrolled spread of genetically modified organisms. Many organic farmers believed that cross fertilisation with GM crops was a real possibility that would lead to them losing their special status and ruin their businesses. More generally environmentalists, conservationists and consumer groups were concerned that GM would lead to a more intensive system of agriculture that would be damaging to wildlife, the environment and to consumer choice.

As the issue began to rise up the political agenda in the summer of 1998, attacks on GM crop trials took place. From March 1998 onwards, a group called Genetix Snowball had masterminded a large number of attacks, which continued throughout 1998 and into 1999. Other

groups such as Greenpeace also undertook direct action to get the message across. These activities included preventing ships carrying GM food from docking, and dumping GM food outside Downing Street, as well as protests at the trial sites. The main purpose was to get publicity for the cause and to keep the issue on the agenda rather than to physically stop the field trials or importation of GM food. However, many farmers became increasingly worried by these attacks and voluntarily gave up the trials. Others were concerned about the effect of bad publicity on their commercial produce, particularly where they produced organic as well as GM food. Meanwhile other groups such as Genewatch and Friends of the Earth, while not undertaking direct action, sought to promote greater public awareness of the dangers of GM food.

The issue was taken up by the media during 1998 and 1999 leading to widespread public alarm during late 1998 and 1999. The term 'Frankenstein Food' was coined. Interestingly, the credit for this emotive phrase goes not to an environmentalist or a tabloid editor but to Malcolm Walker the Chief Executive of the supermarket chain, Iceland, which has often in the past stolen a march on its rivals by adopting a speedy response to consumer health fears about food. Fearing a boycott of their products by consumers, other food retailers began to adopt a policy of GM free foods for their own brands. Meanwhile, food manufacturers also began to reject GM ingredients. Local authorities also imposed bans on GM ingredients in school meals and old people's homes. Then in June 1999 the anti-GM campaigners were delighted when Prince Charles publicly voiced fears about GM technologies in the columns of the *Daily Mail*. Although this was not the first time he had publicly questioned these technologies, his comments now came at a very sensitive time. The Blair government had recently criticised the press and anti-GM campaigners for being hysterical about the issue. Indeed Tony Blair himself referred to the tyranny of environmental pressure groups on this issue.

Although the government resisted the pressure to restrict GM technologies and tried to reassure the public by issuing a special report by its Chief Medical Officer and Chief Scientist, it knew that it had to make concessions. Ministers emphasised that the protection of people and the environment was a priority. The government introduced mandatory labelling of all GM foods sold in shops, takeaways and restaurants. It also reviewed the biotechnology sector and set up a Commission to advise on GM food which, ministers stated, could include environmentalists, consumers and doctors, and not just scientists. The government also sought a voluntary agreement with GM producers not to grow GM foods commercially until field trials had been fully evaluated. This led to an agreement that there would be no general unrestricted cultivation of GM crops until farm trial evaluations were completed. It was expected that the evaluation of herbicide tolerant crops (the ones most likely to be developed commercially in

the next few years) would take four years to evaluate. Moreover, conservation interests are represented on the steering committee monitoring this research. Although not banning commercial development this effectively meant that in effect this would probably be delayed (though most environmental groups were by now calling for a five year moratorium, which the government did not support). Furthermore in June 1999 following a critical report on the possibility of contamination by GM crops, a review of guidelines on farm trials was announced and interestingly, organic groups and environmentalists were invited to contribute to this process. Meanwhile new guidelines on the planting of GM trial crops were introduced, requiring tighter controls to avoid cross-pollination. As a footnote to this, in March 2000, Blair himself acknowledged that fears about GM food were legitimate and that the safety of these foods had to be proved more conclusively.

Pressure groups are obviously keen to make sure they get maximum coverage in a way that is advantageous to their cause or interest. They means that they will criticise unhelpful media coverage. Groups often complain to the broadcasting and press complaints councils about the content of coverage. They also complain to advertising standards bodies about opponents' campaigns. Pressure groups also complain about non-coverage. An example of this occurred in February 2000 when a group of charities including Oxfam, the Worldwide Fund for Nature and Christian Aid, criticised British broadcasters for failing to give what they saw as adequate coverage to international affairs. Research commissioned by the groups found that the amount of factual programmes on international issues dropped by 42%, and on Third World countries by half, over the previous ten years.

Media attention can be invaluable. To under-resourced groups it can be a relatively cheap way of building public awareness. But success is far from guaranteed. Media campaigns can be ineffective and may backfire. Even expensive PR campaigns, like any advertising campaign, can fail miserably. Campaigns may stir public opposition rather than support. Furthermore, on their own, as mentioned, media attention and public support are rarely sufficient to generate government action. Pressure groups will need to make sure that the message gets through to the key decision makers, ministers, civil servants and their advisors. On some issues good contacts with Parliament may also be vital. Media campaigns which lack a political strategy, that do not attempt to build support among decision makers, will tend to fail.

Links with parties

Some pressure groups have traditionally been closely allied to one political party. For example business interests and the Conservative Party, the trade unions and the Labour Party. Other groups have also tended to side with one party for ideological reasons, or because of an overlap of membership, or because that party's policies appear more sympathetic to and compatible with the group's aims. Hence CND has been closely allied with both the Liberal and Labour Party.

In the era of consensus politics, when the two major parties tended to rotate in and out of office , most pressure groups studiously avoided exclusive contact with one political party. They feared that other parties might see them as hostile and could be reluctant to work with them once in office. Nevertheless when one party dominates the political scene, as the Conservatives did between 1979-97 and as Labour threaten to do at the time writing, pressure groups may be less inhibited by these fears. Indeed in the 1980s and 1990s most groups close to the Conservative party enjoyed a great deal of influence . These include business organisations, companies, and trade associations. Also the rightwing think tanks, such as the Adam Smith Institute, the Centre for Policy Studies, and the Institute of Economic Affairs, were very influential in this period.

For many of these groups, efforts to influence the government was like pushing at an open door. Ministers are on the whole were receptive to their ideas. An example was PULSE, a group which sought to encourage competitive tendering and privatisation in the provision of public services. Since the early 1980s this group was warmly received by ministers who readily applied its ideas in central and local government and in the NHS. It was also extremely influential over the details of policy. On several occasions PULSE persuaded the government to amend competitive tendering rules in favour of the private contractors.

Companies which helped to finance the Conservative Party exerted considerable influence over policy during 1980s and 1990s. British Airways was a major donor to Conservative Party funds after privatisation and is generally regarded as having a great deal of influence over policy. This is not to suggest that such donations directly buys influence. The support expressed by such donations creates a sensitivity towards the needs of the donor rather than an obligation to give them exactly what they want. Even so, it is interesting to note that British Airways reduced its donations in 1991 following a series of policy decisions which the company perceived as adverse.

But not all business groups were equally influential in this period. During the 1980s the Confederation of British Industry (CBI) appeared to lose influence. In the early eighties the CBI openly confronted the Thatcher government on a number of economic policy issues, in particular interest rate and exchange rate policies. Other business groups, which were less moderate and more committed to Thatcherism, such as the Institute of Directors (IOD), appeared to have more clout than the CBI during the 1980s.

For many of those pressure groups linked to the Labour Party, the period 1979-96 was nothing short of disastrous. The trade unions lost influence. In addition campaigning groups sympathetic to socialist values, such as Shelter, the Child Poverty Action Group, and so on, found it more difficult to get their arguments across. The same applied to public sector professional groups, representing nurses, doctors, teachers and so on which were often opposed to government policies on the public sector. Nevertheless these groups continued to try and influence policy either through contacts with civil servants, through Parliament, through European institutions (see exhibit four), and by opening channels of communications with Conservative MPs (including some ministers) who were more open to persuasion than others.

During the 1990s it became more and more likely that Labour would form the next Government. Even before the victory at the polls in 1997, groups connected with the Conservatives began to hedge their bets. Some business organisations offered money to the party. Others sought to build bridges in other ways, by meeting Opposition representatives. Before the Blair Government was elected, channels for the representation of interests were already being developed. Following the election of New Labour, business interests have continued to work with government. Though it should be mentioned that the Blair Government has perhaps has been more open to business ideas anyway than previous Labour Governments.

In contrast it has been argued that trade unions have not enjoyed a restoration of the kind of influence that they had under previous Labour Governments. The Blair Government has made some concessions to them, however. In its first term it introduced a minimum wage, new workers' rights with regard to dismissal and leave, New Deals to combat employment, and rights for unions to be recognised by employers. But some of these policies have been criticised by trade unionists for not going far enough. They have argued that the minimum wage was set at a fairly low level, the extension of workers' rights is fairly minimal, and that the New Deals are no substitute for proper jobs.

However, it is perhaps still to early to come to a detailed assessment of the influence of trade unions. Notably the employers have complained that unions now have too much influence over government policy. One should also be careful not to exaggerate the influence of the unions over Labour government before Blair. Labour ministers in the post war period did override the wishes of the unions on many policies. And the relationship was not always cosy. In the late 1960s and again during the 1970s the unions and the Labour Government fought on a number of issues including trade union regulation and incomes policy.

CONCLUSION

Pressure groups can establish a range of political contacts. Generally speaking, good contacts with the executive are the most sought after, though groups ignore the media and Parliament at their peril. The role of political lobbyists is less difficult to evaluate, and some feel that their influence has been exaggerated. In recent years there has been greater pressure for more openness in the dealings between groups and decision-makers and opinion formers. Given the importance of these relationships in the development of policies these pressures can be expected to continue in the future.

The political environment

INTRODUCTION

A wide range of circumstances within the political environment affects the ability of a pressure group to influence policy. It is impossible to discuss them all here. Instead the focus is upon four main factors within the political environment: the compatibility of the group's aims with government policy and the ideology of the governing party; the extent to which government depends upon the group and its members in key policy areas; and finally, the level of electoral and Parliamentary support for the government, the style of government and in particular its willingness to consult outside organisations.

ASK YOURSELF

- How does the wider political context affect the ability of pressure groups to influence policy?
- How has the style and policy programme of successive governments affected relationships with (a) pressure groups in general (b) specific groups?
- In what sense is government dependent on pressure groups?

MAIN TEXT

Compatibility

Generally a pressure group will be more successful if its aims are compatible with current political agendas. If the issues with which the group is concerned are not prominent it will have difficulty getting the public and potential allies, to take notice. In particular the government's own agenda is extremely important because it has a direct impact on policy making. Groups seeking to influence policy must be able to demonstrate at least some compatibility with this agenda. Many groups, even some which have been previously credited with considerable political and economic leverage, have found that on key issues their position was incompatible with the government's agenda. For example during the 1980s and 1990s, powerful groups such as the BMA and the NFU experienced the ignominy of having their views ignored. For example, during this period the BMA's opposition to market style reforms of the NHS was overridden[1]. Even though relationships improved in the honeymoon period after the Blair Government came to office, the BMA has been in dispute with it on a range of issues including funding and performance measurement.

Dependence

During this century government has increasingly relied on pressure groups for a variety of things including advice, support for government policies, and help with implementation of specific policies. As the state's activities expanded, more and more groups became involved and to some extent a mutual dependency was created. The government was able to offer groups some influence over policy in return for their co-operation leverage over the government. Some, particularly those on the right, believed that this was dangerous and could undermine democractically elected governments (see below).

The Thatcher government's (and to some extent the Major government's) attempts to roll back the state and to abandon the interventionist economic policies pursued since the war was partly aimed at reducing its dependence on many groups, notably the trade unions [2]. Similarly the increasing centralisation of matters such as education, housing and urban development was aimed at reducing dependence on the local authorities. However, the outcome was not so simple. For although these groups were now weaker and their views could be given less weight or even ignored in the policy making process, their co-operation was still needed to some degree in policy implementation. Moreover government became more dependent on other groups such as right wing think tanks like the Adam Smith Institute which provided it with alternative expertise and ideas. Also organisations such as management consultants, merchant banks, advertising interests were drawn into the implementation of policies in areas such as privatisation.

But as the government came to rely on such groups, they too began to enjoy the benefits of access to the highest echelons of decision-making. Their role in helping the government enabled them to build contacts which could be useful when they wished to influence government policy. Hence business interests were able to use these channels to lobbying for further changes in the organisation of public sector services which were likely to benefit them directly. For example, during the early eighties management consultancy firms used their high level contacts to press for civil service management reforms which would in turn create a demand for their services.

The government also became more dependent on the voluntary sector. The government's encouragement of voluntary organisations to take over services provided directly by the state has unwittingly financed an expansion of pressure group politics. The government relied on the voluntary sector to deliver services, but its role is wider than this. Voluntary organisations also have a representative role and have sought to maximise the opportunities of access in the decision making process which have arisen from their expanding role in service provision.

Electoral and parliamentary factors

Arguably one of the key factors affecting pressure group politics is the size of government majorities in the House of Commons. In the 1980s the large majorities enjoyed by the Thatcher government minimised the impact of backbench rebellions and enabled the government to get tough with pressure groups, even where there was considerable public support for them.

Other evidence suggests that any changes in the political environment of the 1980s had a marginal impact on most well established relationships between government and pressure groups. Most groups, those who ministers neither regarded as hostile nor as allies, were largely unaffected. The main impact of the government's style and approach was upon the trade unions and public sector professional associations. A survey showed that two thirds of such groups reported a decline in contact with the Prime Minister during the 1980s and 40% reported less contact at ministerial level[3].

But even though some pressure groups were clearly out of favour in the 1980s, this does not necessarily mean they totally lacked influence. Many groups were excluded or ignored when policies were made. But some did not give in, but continued to lobby for changes to the policy as it was implemented. This strategy was pursued by the teaching unions, for example, who managed to secure a number of changes to the national curriculum and assessment system heralded by the 1988 Education Reform Act. A similar approach was taken by the doctors following the introduction of the NHS internal market . The BMA and the Royal Colleges of Medicine protested that the new system would lead to a two tier health service. Subsequently the government introduced rules governing the admission of patients into hospital to reassure the public that those who needed treatment more urgently were given priority. Exhibit ten discusses the role of groups in health policy more generally.

Exhibit ten
Pressure groups and health policy

It is useful to apply the frameworks of analysis outlined in this book to a specific sector of pressure group activity. Health policy for example can be understood to some extent by looking at the various pressure groups involved, how they interact and how they seek to influence the policy process.

Types of group
There are various different types of health pressure group. For example, there are sectional or interest groups, such as doctors' associations (eg: the BMA, the Royal College of Physicians, the Royal College of Surgeons); nurses' associations (eg: the Royal College of Nursing, the Royal College of Midwives, the Community and District Nursing Association) Other professional associations (eg: British Dental Association, National Pharmacists Association); commercial interests and independent health care providers (eg: Independent Healthcare Association, Association of British Health Care Industries, Association of British Pharmaceutical Industry); patients' associations (eg: The Long Term Medical Conditions Alliance; the Patients' Association, the Multiple Sclerosis Society); NHS associations (eg: NHS Confederation, NHS Primary Group Alliance, Association of Community Health Councils in England and Wales).

There are also charities (other than patients groups) which have an interest in health issues, such as Age Concern and the Imperial Cancer Research Fund. Furthermore there are cause groups which campaign on public health issues, such as Action on Smoking and Health; the Food Commission and the UK Public Health Alliance.

In fact there are hundreds of groups interested in health policy. Some are local, such as campaigns to save a local hospital or community health centre. It should also be noted

---

that health policy often involves groups whose core interest lies elsewhere. Environmental groups, safety organisations, and the tobacco and drinks industries to name a few, are all interested to some extent in health matters.

Which are the most influential groups?

Certainly the doctors' organisations appear to be among the most influential groups. They have many resources: public status and respect, expertise, large memberships, financial resources and expertise. They have good contacts with government , Parliament and the media. There is scope for internal conflict, for example GPs often have very different interests from the consultants. Moreover, there are a number of medical organisations in the field, all seeking to present the views of doctors and this could be a potential recipe for division. But generally the medical profession is very good at speaking with a united voice particularly on key issues such as the regulation of doctors, the freedom of doctors to make clinical

decisions, training and remuneration.

Other professional bodies tend to carry less weight, though on areas where their expertise is highly valued they can be very effective indeed. Hence on issues concerning dentistry the British Dental Association is regarded as having much influence. Nurses are a bit of a conundrum. They are well organised, though split between a number of representative groups including the Royal College of Nursing and the trade union, Unison. They have enormous support and respect from the public and have good contacts with government, Parliament and the media. But they are regarded as relatively weak in terms of political influence. It has been argued that is because most nurses are female, while politics is male dominated, but this is surely an over-simplification. It is more the case that nurses have traditionally been seen as junior to doctors and as a result have had less of a presence on key decision making bodies. There are signs that this is changing and it is notable that in

recent years nurses have been more influential on policy issues such as nurse prescribing, the introduction of specialist nursing grades, and the reform of nurse training.

The health service employs many types of staff many of whom are also in trade unions such as Unison. In the 1970s the trade unions were very powerful in the NHS, largely through the threat of disruption brought by industrial action. But their position weakened in the 1980s and 1990s with the passage of trade union legislation. In addition the introduction of competitive tendering in the NHS (and elsewhere in the public sector) led to the replacement of union labour with non-unionised workers. Such competition (combined with the threat of unemployment) further discouraged members from industrial actions.

Commercial interests can exert a lot of influence on health policy. Government support for privately funded hospital programmes and private health insurance has given organisations which have expertise in these fields greater opportunities to present their views. The drugs industry also has a close relationship with government. Government needs the industry to develop new effective drugs and also recognises that the industry is a major employer and exporter. But the drugs industry depends on government to approve drugs, fund drug treatments on the NHS and support university research into pharmaceuticals. Other commercial interests whose activities have implications for health and illness have also been drawn into a relationship with government. These include the drinks industry (alcohol abuse is linked to a range of health and social problems), tobacco (in view of the health problems associated with smoking), and the food industry (diet is an important factor in good health). These are all major industries whose profitability could be damaged by health policies which sought to control or restrict their products. They therefore have an enormous incentive to lobby government, But by the same token government

depends on them for their economic contribution and for their assistance in implementing health policy. Hence the drinks industry can help create conditions for sensible drinking while the food industry can help promote healthy diets.

Organisations that represent NHS bodies also seek to influence the policy process. They have insider status because of their members are statutory bodies and have a lot of knowledge of NHS management and administrative issues and know what is happening 'on the ground'. As well as presenting their views within the hierarchical structure of the NHS, the various statutory organisations have their own representative associations to influence national policy making. For example, health authorities, community health councils and local primary health care groups all have national organisations. But it is argued that these organsations are limited to some extent by the fact that government funds their member organisations. creating a dependency that may

inhibit them from criticising government policy too much.

Patient organisations are relatively weak. This is partly because patients are also traditionally weak relative to professionals. In recent years, the greater emphasis on consumerism and the empowerment of service users has strengthened the position of patients' organisations (and those representing relatives and carers of the sick). Some are now represented on advisory committees and task forces in the Department of Health for example. Most have built up links with Parliament and the media. However, they are relatively under-resourced and have little leverage within the policy process compared with the more established professional and commercial interests.

Voluntary organisations and charities in the health field can carry substantial weight, particular where they are large and have significant independent resources. Examples include the Imperial Cancer Research Fund and Macmillan Cancer Relief. These organisations have access to government and are very influential. Smaller organisations, particularly those that are dependent on government grants are in a weak position and exert correspondingly less influence.

As in other areas of policy making one finds single issue cause groups. These campaign on a range of issues such as smoking, for example. Sometimes they ally with other groups, such as professional associations or patients' groups. In some cases they also join with groups which have a much broader agenda, for example, the environmental pressure groups on issues such as the health effects of pollution. Generally, cause groups in the health field are not regarded as very influential. However, if they can secure the support of other interests, they can exert some influence. For example, on the smoking issue, Action on Smoking and Health has joined forces with the BMA and the Royal College of Physicians to combat smoking. Although the tobacco industry is itself powerful, the anti-smoking lobby has won a

government commitment to ban tobacco advertising and sponsorship.

What are the key factors in determining the influence of health pressure groups in the policy process?

It appears that there are several key factors. First, public support. Health is always at or near the top of the list of public concerns. But some health issues get more coverage than others. There seems to be less sympathy for elderly sufferers from long term chronic conditions. Mental illness too tends to get little public sympathy. In these areas campaigners are faced with a real task of educating the public. The media obviously have an important role in this. Notably the profile of bowel cancer rose following media coverage of the case of Bobby Moore, the former captain of the England football team, who died from the disease. Meanwhile on the issue of mental health, although there is more coverage of these issues in the media than once was the case, mental health pressure groups are constantly fighting against the stereotype of

the 'lunatic killer' which tends to be portrayed in the press. It should be noted that most people who suffer from mental illness suffer from anxiety, depression and neurosis rather than psychotic disorders which lead them to kill.

Secondly, an alliance of groups across the different interests is important. Where agreement can be reached between professional groups, commercial interests, patients' organisations, cause groups and NHS bodies, this creates a powerful momentum. The Blair Government's decision in March 2000 to substantially increase funding for the health service reflected the strength of the coalition of support for extra finding and the level of public support for this, backed by the media.

The government's health agenda is crucial. If a group finds its aims incompatible with this agenda it will have great difficulty influencing policy. For example in the 1980s even the BMA found itself being ignored by government because it opposed the introduction of a market system in the NHS. The Blair Government's policy priorities focus on four main areas: cancer, heart disease, mental illness and accidents. Groups which are campaigning in these areas are to some extent pushing at an open door, But this has obvious implications for those campaigning on issues which affect smaller minorities. Nonetheless, the government has attempted to correct this to some extent by developing policies on ethnic minority health and the health of poorer people in society.

Some issues are perennial on the health agenda. Hence groups concerned about privatisation, rationing, funding the health service and NHS reorganisation find it relatively easy to air their views in the media. Groups interested in these issues are advantaged compared with those trying to raise the profile of other issues. In the past public health issues have attracted less attention than health service issues. However, with the series of crises in the last few decades such as AIDS, BSE, GM food and so on, these kinds of issues are now firmly on the agenda. It is now much easier for groups concerned about social, economic or environmental issues related to health, to raise public and media awareness and put pressure on government to do something about the problem.

The importance of good political contacts with government and Parliament cannot be over-emphasised. In particular groups need to have good links with the Department of Health. It is important they are represented on key advisory committee and task forces and get access to officials and ministers when the need arises. Parliamentary links have become more important in recent years. Now there are many all party groups on health issues, such as cancer for example. There is also a Health Select committee which which reports on issues of contmeporary importance, and which takes evidence from health pressure groups. Other Parliamentary committees also take an interest in health issues including the Commons' Agriculture Committee and Environment, Transport and Regional Affairs Committee, and the House of Lords' Committee on Science and Technology.

Finally, one should not ignore the European dimension. The European Union now has significant powers to encourage the promotion of health. It cannot interfere directly with individual countries' health systems though it can promote various activities through grants and by regulating activities harmful to health. In recent years the EU has funded health research and has taken steps to harmonise controls in order to prevent harm from tobacco and drugs. It also sought to combat health hazards in the workplace and the environment and has intervened in the issue of food safety. It is expected that the EU's health role will expand considerably in the future.

Further reading : see [4]

These groups began to reassert themselves under the Major Government. This was not because this government was particularly keen to hear their views but because it was much more vulnerable to backbench rebellion. From 1992 the Major Government had a small and diminishing majority –and at one point governed with a minority of MPs. In order to get its proposals through Parliament it had to be more open to compromise[5].

Style

During the Thatcher era it appeared that not only were the views of many pressure groups incompatible with government policy, but also that the right of groups even to have their say was incompatible with the Thatcher government's style. Margaret Thatcher and some of her ministers made some scathing comments about pressure groups, particularly the trade unions.

Mrs Thatcher was essentially a conviction politician. In general she saw pressure groups as self-interested organisations. To bargain and negotiate with such groups was the hallmark of corporatism and consensus politics, to which Thatcher attributed the failure of postwar Britain. Her preference was for strong government, defending her interpretation of what was right for Britain against the narrow private interests of pressure groups. This was reflected in a number of ways. Under her leadership the number of advisory committees (see above) fell from 1485 to 971. And although the annual number of consultative documents issued increased under the Thatcher Government (from 38 under Callaghan to 171 under Thatcher), there is evidence to suggest that consultation periods were too short for meaningful consultation to take place [6]. An analysis of a sample of consultative documents in 1998/9 found that the average consultation period was only 39.2 days and that over 60 per cent had deadlines for comment of 40 days or less [7]. But despite the anti-corporatist perspective of the Thatcher Government, concessions and compromises were still made. Some pressure groups were excluded, but others, particularly those allied or sympathetic to Conservative Party, such as the right wing think tanks mentioned earlier, increased their access to the decision-making process. But this wasn't simply because their aims were compatible with government policy. In some cases (for example privatisation, mentioned above) the government also relied on these groups to help deliver its policies. However, as already noted, the necessity for consulting groups over the implementation of policy also brought the government into contact with groups which had either been excluded from prior consultation or which had been unable to exert much influence at this earlier stage.

The appointment of John Major as Thatcher's successor was heralded as a return the more consensual politics of the post war period. Not only was his professed style more inclusive and consensual he was also from 1992 faced with a small Parliamentary majority which placed a premium on compromise. Nonetheless, there was little evidence of a sea change in the style of government. Early evidence did reveal that over a third of groups believed the Major Government to be more open and consultative. However, it also revealed that almost half experienced little change in either the frequency or effectiveness of their contacts with ministers and civil servants[8]. Furthermore, it must be recalled that this was a pre-election period and that the government was doing its best to create an image of a caring and listening administration.

Evidence from the Major period shows a slight increase in the length of consultation periods compared with the Thatcher era. A sample from 1993/4 session of Parliament had an average consultation period of 40.7 days, and the number of documents requesting comments within 40 days was 53 per cent [9]. A later sample from 1995/6 revealed an average of 43.9 days and an even smaller proportion of documents having a consultation period of 40 days or less (50%). More consultative documents per annum were produced under Major than Thatcher, 284 per annum compared with 171. Obviously this is very limited evidence but it does suggest a slightly more open attitude to consultation. The number of advisory committees continued to fall from 971 in 1990 to 610 in 1997, though this excluded a number of ad hoc working parties and expert groups which it appeared were being used as an alternative. There is anecdotal evidence from case studies which illustrate how the Major government excluded important groups from consultation in similar ways as its predecessor, the trade unions being a classic example. But also key professional groups such as the BMA continued to claim that they were excluded from the policy formation process. A quantitative analysis of the relationship between the BMA and the Department of Health found a decline in meetings on policy of around 25%. Meanwhile the proportion of recorded meetings initiated by the government fell from 41% to 30 % between 1980-90 and 1991-95[10].

The Major government was more willing to make concessions in the face of protest than its predecessor, though this is hardly surprising in view of its relatively small majority. One can cite a number of issues in this period, such as testing in schools, the pit closure programme, reforming the police force, to a name a few, where the government apparently conceded ground. But despite its greater willingness to make concessions, the Major government still pursued a programme largely inherited from its predecessor: privatisation, welfare state reform, trade union reform, deregulation. This brought it into conflict with many pressure groups fundamentally opposed to this approach. This alone made it difficult to return to a consensual decision-making style of government and to re-establish partnerships between government and some groups.

Moreover, despite criticism of Major's leadership from the media (not to mention from his predecessor!) his government did not shy from taking on pressure groups in a fairly combative and confrontational manner. A good example of this was its policy on school tests. Some concessions were made in 1991, but these did not satisfy the teaching unions who threatened a boycott. The government responded by confronting the teachers, but had to back down in the face of a successful boycott of the tests in 1993.

What about the style of the Blair Government?

At first sight the philosophy of the Blair Government suggested a return to a genuinely more open and consultative style of government. Groups which had lost influence in the 1980s and 1990s – doctors and teachers included - were offered a more inclusive approach to policy-making in their respective fields. There was anecdotal evidence that groups that had not enjoyed a close relationship with government during the Thatcher and Major periods were now being involved, such as Stonewall, the Low Pay Unit, and Shelter. It also appeared as one observer put it that 'Labour likes people on the inside of the tent' (see [11]).

The Blair Government declared that it would improve policy making by among other things 'consulting outside experts, those who implement policy and those affected by it' [12]. In addition guidance was issued on how to conduct written consultation exercises in 1998. This was introduced in attempt to encourage good practice. The document stated :

'It is important to build consultation with outside interests into plans for policy development, both on specific proposals and services, and more generally. Consultation will help lead to more realistic and robust policy , better reflecting peoples' needs and wishes' [13]. This was welcomed by many pressure groups who saw in it greater opportunities to be consulted. In the first full year of the Blair Administration (1998), 34 Green Papers and 391 other consultative documents were issued. This figure was considerably higher than found under previous governments. However, it must be emphasised that it only related to only one year and could be explained to some extent by the large number of policy initiatives in this period. As far as consultation periods are concerned there was some indication that the Blair Government was performing better than its predecessors in allowing longer time for comments. Analysis of a sample of Green Papers and other consultative documents issued in a six month period from December 1st 1998 and 31 May 1999 found that the average length of consultation was 45.5 days, longer than samples discussed earlier taken during the Thatcher and Major periods. Also the percentage of documents with a deadline for comments of 40 days or less was 45%, less than the Major and Thatcher samples, again suggesting that more time was being given for comments.

The Blair Government also encouraged the use of draft bills to outline proposals before the legislative process began. In the 1996-97 Parliamentary session, two draft bills were introduced. Three were introduced in 1997-98 and seven in 1998-99. The Blair Government also resurrected the Special Standing Committee procedure for the Immigration and Asylum Bill 1998-99. It also appeared to be more willing to report the outcomes of consultation. For example the various phases of consultation on food safety legislation were accompanied by reports on the comments of interested groups and how government had responded to these comments.

But other signs pointed towards less consultation. The number of advisory committees continued to fall, from 610 in 1997 to 544. This was offset to some degree by the creation of task forces to review policy issues. However, as noted earlier there was extensive criticism of the composition of these bodies. Also many task forces were criticised for their lack of openness and rigour in consulting groups. The Blair Government's record has been perhaps slightly better in the appointment of forums and reference groups, though again composition and working methods have been the subject of criticism.

A further point is that the Blair Government has not escaped criticism from some of the groups whom it sought to win over. Both teachers and doctors representatives have expressed their concern about the Blair Government's reforms in the respective fields of education and health and have been particularly annoyed by what they see as failures to consult on new initiatives. Meanwhile welfare groups have been increasingly critical of plans to reforms social security benefits, particularly for single parents, and have claimed that their views have been ignored.

There is also an anti-group philosophy within the Blair government. This was exemplified by Jack Straw, the Home Secretary, who in a newspaper article in 1998 declared that although pressure groups were an important component of democracy, elected politicians should be wary of becoming agents of sectional interests. He went on to say that 'the link between local communities and their elected representatives is worth a thousand pressure groups. It is the basis of our democratic accountability' [14]. Blair made similar comments in February 1999 about anti-GM food campaigners, saying that 'we should resist the tyranny of pressure groups' [15] Indeed the Blair Government was heavily criticised for introducing legislation that defined certain protests as terrorism. The Terrorism Bill, which at the time of writing is passing through its Parliamentary stages, defines terrorism as 'the use or threat, for the purpose of advancing a political religious or ideological cause, of action which involves serious violence against any person or property'. Campaigners were extremely concerned that this broad definition would intimidate protestors who threatened disruption. Other measures in the bill also caused concern including the creation of a new offence of incitement which could inhibit those in the UK campaigning in support of groups fighting oppressive regimes overseas.

CONCLUSION

A variety of factors in the political environment can affect the ability of pressure groups to influence the policy process. Particularly important is the accessibility of government and its willingness to consult with outside organisations. If government does not wish to take account of groups' views and is not prepared to modify its proposals as a result then the opportunities for groups to present their case will be limited. Governments in recent years have adopted very different approaches towards pressure groups. The

Thatcher Government was very combative and appeared distrustful of groups. The Blair Government in contrast has expressed its willingness to be more open and consultative. Clearly the style of government is important. However, it is important to recognise that what the governments says and what it actually does are often very different. Hence the implementation of Thatcher's policies depended on the co-operation and assistance of outside interests while more recently the Blair Government has come under increasing criticism from pressure groups for its failure to consult them fully and modify its proposals in the light of their comments.

Democracy, efficiency and pressure groups

INTRODUCTION

In this final chapter the discussion focuses on the role of pressure groups in a democracy. Although there are many different schools of thought on this role, they can be divided principally into two main camps. On the one hand there are those who see pressure groups as a major contributor to democracy. Then there are others who believe pressure groups undermine democracy. Let us now examine these views in more detail.

ASK YOURSELF

- Do pressure groups enhance democracy or do they undermine it?
- Should government make an effort to work with pressure groups and accommodate their concerns? Why?
- Are pressure groups necessarily self-interested and narrow in their concerns?

MAIN TEXT

Pressure groups represent people. But the type of representation they are involved in differs from that which occurs through the conventional system of electoral or territorial representation which leads to the election of MPs (and councillors at local level) in geographical constituencies. In contrast pressure groups are a form of functional representation. They represent key functions of society, economic, social and administrative. But they also represent a range of preferences in society. Individuals form, support and join groups and they are a legitimate channel through which public preferences are transmitted. Pluralist writers see groups as important to democracy for the following reasons [1];

- They provide a link between the government and the governed. Pressure groups raise issues and bring them to the government's attention. By the same token, a group's interaction with government can enable its members to become better informed about what government is doing in a particular field.
- Pressure groups help to hold government to account. Pressure groups monitor what is going on in their areas of interest and can publicly criticise government if it believes a policy is not appropriate or is failing.
- Pressure groups have a great deal of knowledge and expertise in specific fields of policy. They can contribute to better informed policy debates.
- Pressure groups can assist with the implementation of policy. This can be achieved by highlighting potential problems and pitfalls with policy proposals at an early stage. In some cases the group may be involved in the actual implementation of a policy programme and their members' co-operation is often vital if the policy is to be effective.

Those who adopt the above view tend to make a number of assumption about the pressure group world. They assume that there are no serious impediments to the formation of groups. They assume that although some groups are economically more powerful than others, all groups have at least some resources which they can bring to bear on the policy process. They also assume that groups are responsive to public opinion and can represent these views effectively.

Some have criticised these assumptions[2]. They have argued that the ability of groups to form varies and that the creation of a group does not reflect underlying public support for it. For example the American political scientist, Mancur Olson saw lobbying as a 'public good' available to all, even those who did not contribute to its production. For Olson, interests that were diffused throughout society (such as consumers or taxpayers) faced difficulty in translating into organised groups. Those that did form had to offer special incentives. But this meant that the decision to join a group depended more on these 'special offers' than support for a particular interest, lobby or campaign.

Others have criticised pressure groups for their lack of internal democracy. Few groups have well developed electoral systems to link the rank and file members with the leadership. Even where elections do take place turnout is rather low. In their defence it could be argued that groups are usually in competition with each other, for supporters, members and resources. These competitive pressures should at least make them responsive to public opinion because, it is argued, members/supporters will either desert the group or set up a rival organisation if the original group no longer represents their views. However, critics argue that this is no substitute for internal democratic procedures and that their absence gives group leaders a great deal of scope to misrepresent the views of the rank and file.

Another criticism is that groups undermine economic and social progress. According to this view groups tend to oppose developments such as new roads, industrial installations and power plants, even though these are in the broader public interest. Moreover, professional groups and trade unions are criticised for attempting to block new ways of working and policies which improve the lot of the consumer. More generally groups are seen as distorting the public interest and unnecessarily fuelling public alarm (see [3]). As Dobbs has commented:

Militant pressure groups...rush to judgement exaggerating their case, and expressing themselves in simplistic terms designed for easy headlines they undermine both balanced decision-making and Parliamentary democracy. [4].

A middle way is to appreciate that pressure group representation has both weaknesses and strengths. The weaknesses can be addressed. Greater openness and freedom of information in government would enable groups to hold government to account more effectively. The creation of open forums for consultation on policy would help to create a more level playing field. Encouragement of democratic mechanisms within pressure groups, as has happened with the trade unions in recent years is also a positive step from this perspective. More public funding for interests which have difficulty forming pressure groups, such as consumers for example, is another suggestion.

Pressure groups are valuable political institutions. It has been fashionable in recent years to discount them as vested interests intent on undermining the interests of the public as a whole. However, we must remember that in a democracy the views which pressure groups convey are legitimate interests. Trade unions for example represent around a fifth of the adult population. One cannot simply ignore those who represent such a large proportion of the population. Moreover, not all pressure groups are narrowly self-interested. Cause groups provide an important channel of representation and participation for people with shared values.

Modern democracy would not exist without pressure groups. As a channel of representation, they are as legitimate as the ballot box. Of course, the representativeness of certain groups has been challenged. It is sometimes said that there is no guarantee that pressure group leaders will represent their members' views accurately. But similar questions could be raised about the representativeness of party leaders and of MPs.

Pressure groups can contribute to the efficient running of the state. They can mediate between the government and the governed. Their expertise and knowledge is valuable to policy makers. By co-operating with policies which they have helped form, pressure groups can pave the way for smooth implementation. Pressure groups monitor both new and continuing policies and can provide evidence on its effectiveness and ideas for reform.

It is important to restate the potential contributions of pressure groups, simply because these arguments have been overlooked so much in recent years. Pressure groups have in some cases been regarded as an enemy within, not to be to traded with. Of course government must have direction and leadership. It is also important in a fair society that government helps protect weaker and poorly organised groups from domination or exploitation by the most powerful interests. But this does not provide a good argument for excluding pressure groups from the process of government. While some groups may make unreasonable demands or eschew a close relationship with the state it is nevertheless in the interests of both democratic government and efficient government to try as far as possible to work with pressure groups rather than against them.

References

Chapter one – Welcome to the world of pressure groups

1. Directory of British Associations, London, CBD Research, 1992 (11th edition)
2. K Newton, Second City Politics, Oxford University Press, 1976

Chapter two – Analysing pressure groups

1. R Baggott, 'Pressure Group Politics in Britain: Change and Decline?' *Talking Politics,* 1.1 Autumn 1988, p 25-30
2. A Ball and F Millard, *Pressure Politics in Industrial Societies,* London, Macmillan, 1986, p 334
3. F Castles, *Pressure Groups and Political Culture,* London, Routledge, 1967, p 1
4. G Roberts, *A Dictionary of Political Analysis,* London, Longman, 1971, p 173
5. G Alderman, *Pressure Groups and Government in Great Britain,* London, Longman,1984
6. W Grant, *Pressure Groups, Politics and Democracy in Britain,* London, Philip Allan, 1989, p 9
7. G.Jordan and J.Richardson, *Government and Pressure Groups in Britain,* Oxford, Clarendon Press,1987
8. R Benewick, 'Politics without ideology: the perimeters of pluralism', in R Benewick *Knowledge and Belief in Politics: The Problem of Ideology,* London, Allen and Unwin, 1973
10. M Ryan, *Lobbying From Below,* London, UCL Press, 1996
11 Grant, 1989, p14-15
12 W Maloney, G Jordan, and A McLaughlin (1994), 'Insider Groups and Public Policy: the insider/outsider model revisited', *Journal of Public Policy,* 14(1), p17-38
13. P Whiteley and S Winyard, *Pressure for the Poor: The Poverty Lobby and Policy Making,* London, Methuen, 1987
14. R Baggott, 'The Measurement of Change in Pressure Group Politics', *Talking Politics,* Autumn, 5.1, Autumn 1992, 18-22
15. D Marsh and R Rhodes, *Policy Networks in British Government,* Oxford, Clarendon, 1992; MJ Smith, *Pressure, Power and*

Policy, Hemel Hempstead, Wheatsheaf,1993

16. See for example K Dowding, 'Model or Metaphor? A critical review of the policy network approach', *Political Studies,* 43, p 13-58

17. F Baumgartner and B Jones, *Agendas and Instability in American Politics*, University of Chicago Press, 1993

Chapter Three – Pressure groups and policy making

1. D Toke, 'Power and Environmental Pressure Groups', *Talking Politics,* 9(2), p 107-15; S. Young *The Politics of the Environment,* Baseline Books, Manchester, 1993

2. R Baggott, 'The Measurement of Change in Pressure Group Politics', *Talking Politics,* 5.1, Autumn, 1992, p 18-22

3. J Greenwood, J Grote and K Ronit, *Organised interests and the European Community,* London, Sage, 1992, p 246

Chapter Four – Pressure group resources

1. Whiteley and Winyard, 1987

2. Charity Commission, *Political Activities and Campaigning by Charities* CC9, London, Charity Commission, 1997

3. *The Guardian,* 18 January 2000, p 7

4. *Social Trends, 30,* 2000, p 182

5. R Baggott, 'Nuclear Power at Druridge Bay', Parliamentary Affairs, 51 (3), July 1998, 384-97; B Gubbins, *Power at Bay,* Ryton, Earthright Publications, 1997

6. See F Ridley and G Jordan, 'Protest Politics: Cause Groups and Campaigns', *Parliamentary Affairs* Special Issue, 51(3), 1998 (Oxford University Press, 1998)

7. L Dickson and A McCulloch, 'Shell, the Brent Spar and Greenpeace: A doomed tryst?', *Environmental Politics,* 5(1), 1996, p 122-9

8. G Jordan, 'Politics Without Parties', *Parliamentary Affairs,* 51(3), 1998, p 327

Chapter Five – Pressure group contacts

1. S Platt, *Government By Taskforce: A Review of the Reviews London,* The Catalyst Trust, 1998; A Barker, *Ruling By Task Force: Politico's Guide to Labour's New Elite,* London, Politico's, 1999

2. Cranfield Partnership Research Unit, *The Task Force Revolution*, Bedford, Cranfield University School of Management, 1998

3. A Barnett, *'Firms aren't in Office but are they in power?,* The Observer, 9 April 1998, p 14

4. S Platt, *Government By Taskforce: A Review of the Reviews London,* The Catalyst Trust, 1998

5. Cm 3852, *Our Healthier Nation, London,* The Stationery Office

6. Cm 4386, *Saving Lives Our Healthier Nation,* London, the Stationery Office

7. R Baggott, 'The Measurement of Change in Pressure Group Politics', *Talking Politics,* 5(1), 1992, p 18-22

8. J Burnham, *Whitehall and the Civil Service; Issues for the Millennium and Beyond,* Sheffield Hallam University Press, 2000, p 67-8

9. 'From Chorley to the Charmed Circle', *The Guardian,* 7.7.98, p 3

10. M Rush (ed.), *Parliament and Pressure Politics,* Oxford, Clarendon, 1992

11. R Baggott, 'The Measurement of Change in Pressure Group Politics', *Talking Politics,* 5(1), 1992, p 18-22

12. R Baggott, 'The Measurement of Change in Pressure Group Politics', *Talking Politics,* 5(1), 1992, p18-22

13. C Grantham and I Seymour-Ure, 'Political Consultants', in M Rush (ed) *Parliament and Pressure Politics,* Oxford, Clarendon, 1992, pp 45-85

14. The Guardian, 7 July 1998, p3

15. Reinforcing Standards: Review of the First Report of the Committee on Standards in Public Life, *Sixth Report of the Committee on Standards in*

Public Life, Cm 4557, London, The Stationery Office, 2000

Chapter Six – The political environment

1. Jeremy Lee Potter, *A Damned Bad Business,* London, Gollancz, 1997

2. R Baggott, From 'Consultation to Confrontation:? Pressure Group Relations from Thatcher to Major', *Parliamentary Affairs,* 48 (3), 1995, p 484-502

3. R Baggott, 'The Measurement of Change in Pressure Group Politics', *Talking Politics* 5(1), 1992, p18-22

4. C Ham, *Health Policy in Britain,* Basingstoke, Macmillan, 1999, (4th edition) and R Baggott *Health and Health Care in Britain*, Basingstoke Macmillan, 1998, (2nd edition)

5. R Baggott and V McGregor-Riley, Renewed Consultation or Continued Exclusion? Organised Interests and the Major Governments', in P Dorey (ed), *The Major Premiership: Politics and Policies under John Major 1990-7,* Houndmills, Macmillan, 1999, p 68-86

6. Hansard Society, *Making the Law,* The Report of the Hansard Society on the Legislative Process, London, Hansard Society, 1993

7. Baggott and McGregor-Riley

8. R Baggott, 'The Measurement of Change in Pressure Group

Politics', *Talking Politics,* 5(1), 1992, p18-22

9. Baggott and McGregor-Riley

10. Baggott and McGregor-Riley

11. A Woolf, 'Pressing Problem', *Guardian Society,* 12 May 1999, p 8-9

12. *Modernising Government,* White Paper, Cm 4310, 1999, p 16

13. Service First, Cabinet Office, *How to Conduct Written Consultation Exercises*, London, Cabinet Office, 1998, p 2

14. *The Times*, 8 April 1998, p 16

15. *Electronic Telegraph,* 1366, 20 February 1999

Foundation, 1996, p 22-9

4. M Dobbs, *The Times,* 13 September 1995 p 17

Chapter Seven – Democracy, Efficiency and Pressure Groups

1. For a discussion of the pluralist perspective, see C Brown, 'Pluralism: a lost perspective', *Talking Politics,* 1989, 1(3) 95-100, G Jordan, 'The Pluralism of Pluralism: An Anti-Theory', Political Studies, 1990, p 286-301; and D Wilson, *Pressure: the A to Z of Campaigning in Britain,* London, Heinemann, 1984

2. M Olson, *The Logic of Collective Action,* (Cambridge MA, Harvard University Press); M Pirie *Micropolitics: The Creation of Successful Policy,* (Aldershot, Wildwood House)

3. P Bazalgette, 'When Pressure Groups Get it Wrong', in W Waldegrave et al, Pressure Groups in Modern Britain, London, Social Market

Further Reading

R Baggott, *Pressure Groups Today*, MUP, 1995

W Grant, *Pressure Groups and British Politics,* Macmillan, 2000

B Gubbins, *Power at Bay*, Earthright Publications, 1997

G Jordan and W Maloney, *The Protest Business,* MUP, 1997

D Judge, Representation: Theory and Practice in Britain, Routledge, 1999

F Ridley and G Jordan, 'Protest Politics: Cause Groups and Campaigns', Parliamentary Affairs, Special Issue 51(3) 1998 (Oxford University Press, 1998)

M Ryan, Pressure From Below, UCL Press, 1996

W. Waldegrave, C. Secrett, P. Bazalgette, A.Gaines, K. Parminter, Pressure Group Politics in Britain, London, Social Market Foundation, 1996.

Some possible examination questions

1. Define a pressure group. Why do academics disagree over the definition of pressure groups?

2. Discuss the various approaches to classifying pressure groups. Which approach do you think is the best and why?

3. To what extent does the concept of policy networks further our understanding of pressure group politics and the policy process?

4. What access do pressure groups have to policy making in the UK?

5. In what sense and to what extent do pressure groups influence policy in the UK?

6. To what extent do UK pressure groups focus on European political institutions in an effort to influence domestic government policy?

7. How successful have environmental pressure groups been in influencing government policy in the UK over the last two decades?

8 'Protest is the last resort of a pressure group'. Discuss.

9. Discuss the view that pressure groups representing business have far greater resources at their disposal than those representing labour when engaging in the political process.

10. 'The most important resource a pressure group can have is public support'. Discuss.

11. 'In pressure group politics, organisation is all'. Discuss.

12. In what ways to pressure groups seek to influence (a) the Executive (b) Parliament?

13. Why do major pressure groups concentrate their activities on Whitehall rather than Westminster?

14. What factors do government officials regard as important when dealing with representatives of pressure groups?

15. Are insider groups always more influential over policy than outsider groups?

16. How important to (a) government (b) pressure groups is the consultation process?

17. 'Even the most well-connected pressure groups cannot ignore the media'. Discuss.

18. 'The regulation of MPs interests has gone far enough'. Discuss.

19. Comment on the view that the trade unions close links with the Labour Party has contributed to their decline as a powerful pressure group.

20. 'Many important pressure groups had less access to government between 1979 and 1997 than previously was the case'. Discuss.

21. Comment on the impact of the Blair Government's approach to consultation on pressure group politics.

22. 'Government should not become too dependent on pressure groups'. Discuss.

23. 'The most important thing for a pressure group is its compatibility with the government's agenda'. Discuss.

24. 'Business pressure groups have benefited from the emphasis of both parties on economic growth at any price'. Discuss.

25. 'Pressure groups are undemocratic and therefore bad for democracy'. Discuss.

26. Comment on the view that pressure groups can contribute to the efficient running of the state.

27. 'Far from being suppressed the pressure group system should be extended to cover all possible interests, even those which are currently not well organised'. Discuss.

28. How might government seek to create a fair balance between well organised, wealthy pressure groups and poorly organised, under-resourced pressure groups?

Index

324
4

BAG